Principles for Life

PRINCIPLES FOR LIFE

Robert T. Boyd

WORLD
Bible Publishers, Inc.
Iowa Falls, IA 50126 U.S.A.

Copyright © 1995 by Robert T. Boyd

All rights reserved

The King James Version is used throughout this volume unless otherwise noted.

Credit has been given in the notes for excerpts requiring permission. Mention is made where sources could not be recalled.

ISBN 0-529-11143-8

No part of this publication may be reproduced, stored in a retrieval system, or transmitted, in any form or by any means, electronic, mechanical, photocopying, recording or otherwise, except for brief quotations in critical reviews or articles, without the prior permission of the publisher.

1 2 3 4 5 6 7 8 03 02 01 00

Printed in the United States of America

CONTENTS

Introduction	In God's School of Obedience	xi
Chapter One	The Principle of Bible Study *Second Timothy 2:15*	1
Chapter Two	The Principle of Sacrifice *Leviticus 17:11; Romans 12:1*	15
Chapter Three	The Principle of the Priesthood *First Peter 2:9*	27
Chapter Four	The Principle of Love *Deuteronomy 6:5; First John 4:7*	33
Chapter Five	The Lord's Principle: Sanctification and Leaven *Exodus 13:2,3,9; I Thessalonians 4:3*	41
Chapter Six	The Principle of Forgiveness *Mark 11:25; Ephesians 4:32*	47
Chapter Seven	The Principle of Prayer *Luke 18:1; First Thessalonians 5:17*	55
Chapter Eight	The Principle of Faith *Romans 3:27,28; Hebrews 11:6*	65
Chapter Nine	The Principle of the Harvest *Galatians 6:7,8*	77
Chapter Ten	The Principle of Separation *Romans 12:2; Second Corinthians 6:17*	87
Chapter Eleven	The Principle of Soulwinning *Matthew 4:19; Proverbs 11:30*	99
Chapter Twelve	The Principle of Stewardship *First Corinthians 4:2*	109
Chapter Thirteen	The Principle of Rejoicing and Thanksgiving *Philippians 4:4; First Thessalonians 5:16,18*	115

Chapter Fourteen	**The Principle of the Christian's Warfare** *Second Corinthains; Ephesians 6:11*	125
Chapter Fifteen	**The Principle of Judgment** *Amos 4:12b; Hebrews 9:27; II Corinthians 5:10*	133
Endnotes		145
Bibliography		147

Dedicated to

*Carol Ochs
and
Dan Penwell*

*great helpers in
manuscript preparation*

also

*Marvin and Susan Spencer
Lee and Dorothy Wildey
Bob and Anne Riedmiller*

Good Friends in the Lord

ACKNOWLEDGEMENTS

Many, many thanks to my wife, Peggy, for helping in research.
to Demi Tsiatsos of Martinsburg, WV and
Thelma Ober of DeLand, FL for proofreading.
Also to Rev. Douglas May of Frederick, MD for his computer assistance.

IN GOD'S SCHOOL OF OBEDIENCE
Introduction

The first thing that comes to our minds when *school* is mentioned is a teacher for a given subject and a test to see if we have been obedient in listening to lectures and in studying the text book. Disobedience to educational *laws* will mean failure, a dreadful price to pay in advancement.

Because the human race is a product of Divine creation, man is responsible to His Maker. God, Who as the giver of life, has a right to make laws for his creatures. Adam and Eve were given the privilege of eating fruit from all the trees in the Garden of Eden except one, which was God's. He gave our first parents a law, a choice; "eat of My tree and die" or "do not eat of My tree and live" (Genesis 2:16,17). God does not force anyone to obey Him but it doesn't take man long to learn the error of his way if he is disobedient to God's requirements. Man's way may seem right in his own eyes but the end leads to death (Proverbs 14:12).

Adam was created in God's image and likeness and thus became the federal head of the human race (Genesis 1:26,27). Due to his disobeying God's law in eating of His tree, he died spiritually, becoming a sinner. God made a provision for him to have his standing with him reinstated, but the consequence of his sin caused all his descendants to be born in *his likeness and image*. His spiritual death passed upon them, making each person born thereafter a sinner too (Romans 5:12; Genesis 5:3). King David reminds us of this situation when he said of his birth, "I was brought forth in iniquity and in sin did my mother conceive me' (Psalm 51:5).

Each person born into this world, no matter who or in what country, comes in as a sinner in God's sight. We have all sinned and come short of the glory of God (Romans 3:23). He/she is what God calls a *natural* person, one who has the senses of life, but a mind that is totally foreign to the things of his Creator. "The natural man does not receive the things of the Spirit of God, for they are foolishness unto him, neither can he grasp them because they are of a spiritual nature" (I Corinthians 2:14). However, in spite of the fact that man's heart is deceitful and desperately wicked and walks in the imagination of his own evil heart, there are certain laws in

xi

his mind that prey on his conscience when he does things that just don't seem right (Jeremiah 17:9; 11:8; Romans 2:14).

We notice that one of Adam's sons, Cain, broke an unwritten law, that of *murder*. His brother, Abel, had chosen to obey an unwritten law in offering a proper sacrifice that would meet God's approval, a blood sacrifice of an animal (Genesis 4:1–16). God gave Cain an opportunity to make things right but he refused to obey God's ordained way of offering a proper sacrifice. Jealousy reigned in his heart so he stooped to vent his anger by murdering brother Abel. Sadly, "he went out from the presence of the Lord." For one who seeks to approach the true and living God by *their own way* or *their laws*, Scripture gives a warning, "Woe unto them who go the way of Cain" (Jude 11). We can assume his conscience had become "seared as with a hot iron" (II Timothy 4:2).

We notice at the beginning of time for man that the Bible does not make any list of "laws" for man to follow. According to Paul, "laws" were made by men (Romans 2:14). Although man is evil by nature in thought and deed, he possesses something not found in other creatures. His conscience reveals there is a "higher being" and as a result he seeks to establish a religion that satisfies his own mind. The flood of Noah's day was God's answer to man's thoughts being evil *continually* (Genesis 6:5). It wasn't until the days of Moses that God began to put down *written* laws. The laws of man's heart blinded him to his need of God, so God *added* or had His laws written down for man to know what is right and what is wrong (Galatians 3:19). God's thoughts are not ours and our ways are not His, hence a need to get out His Text Book, the Bible, and learn what we are to do to be obedient to Him.

The laws God gives are established and enforced by His authority and given to the human race as a basic tenet for godly living. "Principle" is the general term signifying a rule laid down or established. It implies a penalty or inconvenience for disobedience. Moses told the children of Israel the blessing that would be theirs if they obeyed God, and what punishment they would have to bear if they disobeyed him (Deuteronony 28). The purpose of God's commands is to give man His best when obeyed.

The Bible is filled with laws that don't begin with a "Don't." For example: Christ said, "Follow Me and I will make you fishers of men" (Matthew 4:19). Obedience and following Him will produce results. A man can gain the whole world but lose his own soul (Mark 8:36). Only obedience to God's requirements will give him salvation of his soul. If sin is confessed, forgiveness is promised (I John 1:9). Confession is a command and unless performed, no forgiveness. In each of these verses a law is present. One can either obey or disobey. In other words, God has us coming or going.

In pointing a finger at God because of His laws, we forget that our government has tens of thousands of laws on its books—laws that its citizens must obey or else. Scientists had to obey certain laws to get a man on the moon. Pilots must follow certain "laws" for a blind landing in the fog or else there is a crash. We have sanitary laws else people would be dying daily. So why downgrade God for laws that help spiritually so that one might avoid a devil's hell and enjoy a happy life as

Introduction xiii

he awaits his home in heaven? None should ever blame God for His laws and the consequences of breaking them. It pays to *observe and do* any and all of His laws—negative and positive—that He makes. If one rebels against the laws of God, he might as well rebel against all the laws of his government. However, if someone breaks a law that affects another, the injured person will rise up in arms and seek revenge or justice. So why do we think we have a right to point an accusing finger at God for His laws and the con-sequences of breaking them?

The big argument against God's "Don't" laws has to do with the Ten Commandments as found in Exodus 20:1–17. Like the retired justice said, "there are no loopholes in them."Once we learn the reason God gave these commandments we can better understand what He sought to get across in giving them to mankind in general. The law was *added* because of man's sinfulness— to reveal to man what he has done that was wrong in God's sight, to *spell* out what sin really is, and to help him see what he should and should not do to please God (Galatians 3:19). Natural man needs to be aware of these laws so that he might be freed from the "idolatry" of any and all religions.

As one reads through this book, he/she will find the purpose i:~ to collie to grips with the truth that to obey is better than any plan one might concoct to find a satisfaction that is permanent. "The wicked are like the troubled sea, when it cannot rest, whose waters cast up mire and dirt. There is *no* peace, the Lord said, to the wicked" (Isaiah 57:20,21). True satisfaction comes when we take God at His Word, observe and do what He says, accept Christ as our very own personal Savior, walk with Him daily as He is in the light, and therein we have a peace that passes all understanding. The relationship between these two is indescribable, and no matter what one thinks otherwise, it pays to observe any law God makes. We may be in the minority, but "if God is for us, who can be against us!" (Romans 8:31).

In the Old Testament there are so many physical laws that pertain only to the nation of Israel, but from Genesis through Revelation, God's word is filled with spiritual laws for His children of all ages to apply to their hearts. "All Scripture is given by inspiration of God and is profitable for doctrine [to make us wise unto salvation], for correction, to rebuke and for instruction in righteousness, that God's child may be mature in all spiritual things" (II Timothy 3:16,17). When we use our text Book and "observe and do" all that God tells us to do as we attend the "School of God," we not only have a personal relationship with our heavenly Father but with our fellow man. With Christ as our personal Savior, keeping God's laws is not only a privilege but a blessing as well.

In the chapters that follow, several laws will be considered in which we will try to cover all that is necessary to make the child of God a well-pleasing servant. Spiritual applications will be given to help us to recognize that God's laws are for our benefit, not only as we live and move and have our being before Him but also before others. In a land that is fast becoming like Sodom and Gomorrah, with laws broken and criminals going free, may God help us to approach His laws with an honest desire to accept them from a loving God who has our best interests at heart. The thought of "observing and doing" is mentioned at least 53 times in the Bible. God only needs to say something once, but when he says something over and over, we better sit up and pay attention. No matter the law, if we willingly keep them, God's mercies will be new every morning, coupled with His faithfulness, which will challenge us to "keep on keeping on" day by day (Lamentations 3:22,23).

> Dear heavenly Father, help me to be so obedient to Your laws that my walk might be worthy of the calling You have given to every believer. Help me to so abide in Christ's will for my life that I might have confidence and not be ashamed before him at His coming. In His wonderful name I pray. Amen.
> (Ephesians 4:1; 1 John 2:28

Principles for Life

Chapter One

THE PRINCIPLE OF BIBLE STUDY
Our Text Book of Obedience

In this chapter we want to consider truths that a believer needs to know from God's Word to do and be all that is expected of him. After we are saved, He leaves us here on earth to abide by His Word as we prepare to meet Him in glory.

The moment one trusts in Christ as their Savior and are born again, they immediately are baptized into the body of Christ by the Holy Spirit and become new creatures in Christ. Old things pass away and all things become new (I Corinthians 12:13; II Corinthians 5:17). They are now servants of God, servants of righteousness. Before they were servants of sin (Romans 6:17,18,22).

God does not save someone just to give them a "one-way ticket" for heaven, just to save them from hell, although that is included in salvation. We are saved to serve Him. He is our new Master and we are His co-laborers (I Corinthians 3:9). As His representatives on earth, we have a specific job to do until He calls us home to live with Him for all eternity.

When we are born again we are "babes in Christ." The regulations and rules He lays out for His children are entirely different from our old way of living, hence as a new born baby needs to grow with proper food, so a new born babe in Christ needs to be nourished for spiritual growth.

Before one became a Christian, his life was under the domain of Satan, but as long as the individual remains a lost sinner, Satan is content to let the person live to suit himself. But when a sinner comes to Jesus and is saved, *look out*! Satan is now ready to start on a rampage to keep this newly saved person from growing into maturity in the things of the Lord. I suggest that this individual go back in his thinking and try to pinpoint the place where he accepted Christ and the time of the transaction. Then when Satan tries to get him to doubt his salvation or questions him if he really did accept Christ as his Savior, he can tell the devil "I was saved in my Church (or wherever) at noon (or the time). I know I was converted then because I was there when it happened!"

Many questions begin to come to mind concerning his new experience in life.

Here are several:

What actually happened to me?
What do I do now that I am a child of God?
How do I grow and develop spiritually?
Will it be possible for me to overcome temptations?
Just what does God expect of me as His child?
Will doubts ever crop up in my mind?
Should I tell people I'm saved or keep it a secret?
What can, and can't I do?
Where can, and can't I go?
What assurance does God give that I am truly His?
Is reading my Bible and praying necessary?
Do I have to give up my old friends and habits?
Will the devil now leave me alone?
Does God have a will for my life?
Should I start going to Church?

Such questions are only natural for a new Christian to ask. It takes time to learn and grow with God's requirements. This step of salvation, which has just been taken is not the end—it is but the beginning of a new life.

One should not try to understand everything at once. A child can talk before it understands the rules of grammar. He cares nothing about the process of digestion and assimilation, only "Let's eat!" Just as a child expresses himself as best he can, learning and growing, sitting, crawling, walking, etc., so we, in our experience as a new-born babe in Christ, must begin to show growth in our walk—things that accompany salvation (Hebrews 6:9). A new Christian should begin to—

Witness immediately to others of your new experience in Christ to saved friends or unsaved friends—anybody. Jesus said "If you confess Me before men I will confess you before My Father who is in heaven. Deny Me and I will deny you before My Father" (Matthew 10:32.33). We are to *tell* and *show* others what great things God has done for us (Mark 5:19; Luke 8:39). The redeemed of the Lord must *say* so (Psalm 107:2). We are assured from Scripture that those who believe on Christ shall not be ashamed or timid (Romans 10:11).

Associate immediately with other Christians. They will be in a good fundamental Bible believing Church, a Church in which you need to become a member. By so doing you become active in the services and their program. The Psalmist said, "I was glad when they said unto me, let us go into the house of the Lord" (Psalm 122:1). A believer cannot be a *loner*, he must not forsake the assembling of himself with other believers (Hebrews 10:25).

Christian fellowship is essential. The new converts should also seek other Christians in their community, at work or in school.

The Principle of Bible Study

As the two upper points are followed immediately after conversion, this Principle becomes a necessity to recognize and obey to prove that one's faith in Christ is real.

The Principle of Bible Study

This Principle is "Study to show yourself approved unto God, a workman [servant] who needs not to be ashamed [of his stand for Christ], but rightly divides the word of truth" (II Timothy 2:15). The "word of truth" (our Bible), has been given to us by inspiration of God and is profitable for doctrine, for reproof, for correction and instruction in righteousness, that the man of God (each believer) may become qualified to do all that God's law requires them to do, thoroughly equipped for every good work (II Timothy 3:16,17).

In enrolling in the "School of God," it is wise to talk with the pastor or Sunday School teacher and ask for suggestions about what portions of Scripture should be studied. John's Gospel is a good Book to start reading and study. A good pastor will give some verses to learn to use in witnessing, verses telling of your need for Christ and your experience in believing on Christ as your Savior. Since there are so many versions and translations of the Bible on the market, ask which Bible to use. I personally would recommend either the New King James Version or the New American Standard edition.

Just as it is impossible to go from one grade to another in school without studying your lesson, a Christian cannot develop and grow and move ahead unless "The Principle of Bible Study" is a daily routine. Just as a baby needs food to grow physically, a Christian needs food to grow spiritually, which is God's Word, the Bible. The following is God's diet:

> *Milk*, for starters. "As new born babes, desire the pure milk of the Word that you may grow in grace and knowledge of your Lord and Savior, Jesus Christ" (I Peter 2:2; II Peter 3:18).
>
> *Bread*. "Man shall not live by bread alone, but by every Word that proceeds out of the mouth of God" (Matthew 4:4).
>
> *Meat*. As one matures, more solid food is needed. If one continues feasting just on milk, he becomes unskilled in the Word and remains a babe. But strong meat belongs to those who become of age, learning to obey God and finding out the consequences of disobedience (Hebrews 5:13,14).
>
> *Dessert*. No meal is complete unless there is something for a "sweet tooth," so God provides the *honey of His Word*. God's Word is sweet to our taste (Psalm 19:7–10; 119:103).

Jeremiah's appetite was satisfied with God's Word for he said His "Word was found and I did *eat* them" (15:16). So did old Job when he said, "I esteemed the Words of His mouth *more* than my necessary food" (23:12). No wonder the Psalmist said, "O taste and see that the Lord is good (34:8). When I finish my third meal for the day, I have to ask, "How many meals did I have today from the Word of God?" Have you ever asked this question and if so, what was your answer?

While feasting on the Word of God, there is a variety of essential verses that should be *memorized*. The Holy Spirit is always present to bring to our remembrance what we need under any circumstance. Always keep in mind that the

Christian life started by faith in Christ and is lived daily by faith (Romans 5:1; Galatians 2:20). The only place we get faith is from the Word of God (Romans 10:17). Our teacher to help us fulfill the "Principle of Bible Study" is the Holy Spirit Himself (John 14:26). Listed are some verses that should be memorized over a period of time.

> Having accepted Christ your own Savior: John 5:23; Ephesians 2:8–10;II Corinthians 5:17.
> When God saved you, you were saved to serve Him: John 15:16; Jude 3; Acts 1:8; Mark 1:17,18.
> Portions of Scripture that will help you in growth and service: Psalm 126:6; Colossians 3:1,2; II Peter 3:18; Romans 1:16; Proverbs 3:5,6; Hebrews 4:16; Matthew 4:19; Proverbs 11:30; Daniel 12:3; I John 2:15–17; II Timothy 2:19; I Corinthians 3:16,17; 6:19,20; Philippians 4:6,13,19; Matthew 26:41; I Corinthians 10:13; Ephesians 6:10–18; II Corinthians 10:3–5; II Timothy 1:13; I Peter 4:12,13; 5:8,9; Titus 2:11–15; Psalm 1:1,2;
> I Thessalonians 5:17,18; I Corinthians 15:10; II Timothy 4:7,8.
> For Victory and Assurance: I John 3:14; 5:1–5,10–12; II Timothy 2:3; Psalm 119:133; Romans 8:28,29 (being conformed to the image of Christ" is the purpose of verse 28); John 5:24.

If in doubt as to what to say, what to do, or where to go: Psalm 119:130; First Corinthians 10:23,31; Colossians 3:17; Romans 14:13; First Peter 2:21; I John 2:28. We must, in all our ways, acknowledge Him and He will direct our path (Proverbs 3:5,6). The steps of a good man are ordered of the Lord
(Psalm 37:23).

As we rely upon God's Word to keep us safe and to use us as His servants we cannot overlook the truth that "Faith without works is dead" (James 2:20). God told Joshua he must *observe* [His Word] and *do* [it], and we must do the same (1:8). See Second Timothy 1:13; First Thessalonians 5:16,19,21 and Jeremiah 48:10a. It is our responsibility to fear the Lord and serve Him in truth (I Samuel 12:24). What we learn and apply God promises us His Word will not return unto Him void, that it will accomplish its purpose and will enable us to prosper (Isaiah 55:11). Dwight L. Moody said, "Sin will keep you from the Bible or the Bible will keep you from sin." In obeying "the Principle of Bible Study" we "walk in the light as He is in the light, having fellowship with God and with one another" (I John 1:7).

As one *digs* into the Word of God and it takes root, the light and the understanding the Holy Spirit gives spurns growth, which results in obedience in ones daily walk. Meeting with spiritual success with each step makes one appreciate all the verses that have been memorized. What a joy it will be to call them to mind when discussing Bible subjects, when witnessing, when needed to solve problems, resist temptation or resist Satan. The more Scripture we know, the easier it is to call upon God for Him to show us great and mighty things (Jeremiah 33:3).

As you study the Scriptures, it is not how many verses or chapters you read. The secret of gaining knowledge is not how much is read but how much is gotten out of what is read even if it is but a few verses at a time. The most important thing is to get to know God's will as revealed in studying.

Search the Scriptures

This is the admonition of none other than Jesus Himself. "Search [study] the Scriptures," He said, "for in them you think you have eternal life, and they are they which testify of Me" (John 5:39). It has been said that the Bible is like a "scarlet thread for no matter where you cut it, it will bleed." Christ is seen in every Book of the Bible and the "scarlet thread" is a symbol of His shed blood in our behalf for our sins. Since we see Christ throughout, the *Subject of the Bible is Redemption* (Ephesians 1:3–14)[1]

It was *proposed* and *planned* by the *Father* in eternity past, for Christ was the *Lamb* slain before the foundation of the world (Revelation 13:8b).

It was *accomplished* by the Son when He gave His life a ransom for sinners (Mark 10:45; Romans 5:6–18).

It was *made known* to us by the *Holy Spirit* when He made known to us our sinful state and revealed to us righteousness for our salvation and judgment if we refuse to believe on Christ (John 16:7–9).

God *thought* it, Christ *wrought* it, the Holy Spirit *brought* it, the devil *fought* it, and thank God, *I got it!*

The Purpose of the Bible:
    To provide a foundation for our faith (Romans 10:17).
    To make us wise unto salvation (II Timothy 3:15).
    To reveal God's overall plan for us and to show His interest in and love for us according to His Word: II Timothy 3:16,17.

The Scriptures were Designed to:
    Testify of Christ and His finished work of redemption for lost mankind: John 5:39; II Corinthians 15:3,4.
    Preach (herald), listen to and apply: James 1:22; Luke 11:28.
    Make us wise (knowledgeable and desirous) for salvation: II Timothy 3:15.
    Produce faith to accept Christ as our Savior: Romans 10:17; 5:1.
    Regenerate us—produce the new birth by the renewing of the Holy Spirit: Titus 3:5; I Peter 1:23; James 1:18.
    Quicken us—keep us awake to our spiritual needs: Psalm 119:50,93; Hebrews 4:12.
    Keep our hearts clean: John 15:3; Psalm 119:9.

Make wise the simple—those who could easily be deceived: Psalm 19:7b; 119:130.

Promote growth—to build one up in the faith: I Peter 2 :2; II Timothy 3:18; Acts 20:32.

Instruct, admonish and reprove: II Timothy 3:16; 4:2; I Corinthians 10:11; Colossians 3:16.

Encourage and produce obedience: Deuteronomy 17:19,20; Jeremiah 38:20.

Keep us from sin: Psalm 119:11; I John 2:1.

Supply our daily spiritual food: Matthew 4:4; Job 23:12; Jeremiah 15:16.

Work effectively in the believer's life: I Thessalonians 2:13.

Comfort in trials: Psalm 119:82.

Sanctify—set apart a believer unto God: Ephesians 5:26; John 17:17.

Offer hope: Psalm 119:49; Romans 15:4.

Provide joy: Psalm 19:8; 119:111.

Examine isms, cults, try every spirit and have Biblical answers to refute them: Isaiah 8:19,20; I John 4:1. We must be like the Bereans: Acts 17:11.

Have full knowledge to be able to give a reason for the hope we have in Christ: I Peter 3:15.

Challenge us to be soul-winners: Luke 8:11–15; Psalm 126:6; Proverbs 11:30; Daniel 12:3.

Make God's children fruit producers: John 15:3,5.

Give victory over Satan: Matthew 4:7,19; Ephesians 6:10–18; James 4:7.

Perfect the man of God: II Timothy 3:17; Colossians 3:16.

Accomplish God's purpose: Isaiah 55:11.

Give us *doctrine*, or the basic principles of Christianity which must be accepted as *valid* and *authoritative*. It involves what is needed for instruction in righteousnes, to reprove and correct for the purpose of producing godly living on a daily basis (II Timothy 3:16,7). Doctrine is essential for every believer, and for Churches to have a doctrinal statement based, not on how Denominations interpret Scripture or link traditions with it but by what the Holy Bible itself says.

Bible Doctrine. There must be the belief that—

1. All Scripture from Genesis 1:1 through Revelation 22:21 is divinely *inspired* of God. Check these verses: Exodus 4:15; II Samuel 23:2,3; Isaiah 59:21; Jeremiah 1:9; and many, many other verses where the phrase, "Thus says the Lord" is used. Christ put His stamp of approval on the Old Testament in Matthew 5:18; 22:42,43; Mark 12:36 and John 10:35. Paul used the expression "it is written" no less than 43 times in referring to the Scriptures of his day. He let us know that Christ died for our sins, was buried and raised from the dead the third day *according to the Scriptures* (I Corinthians 15:3,4). In the New Testament we find that Christ, who is "the Word," spoke to us in His day (Hebrews 1:1,2) and Paul includes the New Testament by saying that *all* Scripture is inspired of God (John 1:1,2; II Timothy 3:16,17).

2. A belief that God is *three* Persons in one. Moses tells us that "The Lord our God is one God" (Deuteronomy 6:4). True, but when He created the heavens and

the earth, God is referred to as *Elohim*, which title is *plural* as we note when He created man He said "let *us* [plural] make man" (Genesis 1:26). In the Godhead we find *God the Father* (John 6:27), *Christ, the Son of God*, Deity, God-Man, God incarnate (John 10:36; I Timothy 3:16) and the *Holy Spirit* who is God and referred to as the third Person of the Trinity. He is our Comforter and Teacher (Acts 5:3,4; John 14:26).

3. The *virgin* birth of Christ, conceived by the Holy Spirit, not by man but with a body prepared by God—God/Man (Matthew 1:18–25; Hebrews 10:5).

He is the sinless, spotless Son of God. Though He was tempted in all points such as we, He did not sin (Hebrews 4;15).

There are some who think that because Christ was tempted by Satan He could have sinned, else why was He tempted. We might as well say that because an army cannot be defeated, it cannot be attacked. The answer is obvious; the Spirit led Him into the wilderness to show that He was Almighty, Lord and Master of all things, that Satan could not master Him.

Christ was not only sinless, he was impeccable—that is, incapable of sinning. This is why He was born of a virgin, conceived by the Holy Spirit, and possessing a body which was prepared by God, not a body with a sinful nature and an earthly father (Hebrews 10:5). He is equal with God, but for the sins of the world He took upon Himself the form (not nature) of man, making of Himself no reputation as lie became a servant, made in the likeness of man (Philippians 2:6,7).

> He was without sin: Hebrews 4:15.
> He did no sin: I Peter 2:22.
> In Him was no sin: I John 3:5. Contrast with verse eight.
> He knew no sin: II Corinthians 5:21
> He was holy, undefiled, separate from sinners: Matthew 7:26.

God permitted Jesus to be tempted if for no other reason than to demonstrate His impeccability. There was absolutely nothing in His whole make up that would or could succumb to sin. Throw a lighted match into a barrel of gunpowder and it will explode. Why? Because it is susceptible to fire. Throw a lighted match into a bucket of water and the fire is quenched. Why? Because water has nothing in it that is susceptible to fire. Satan can find something is us that will result in sin but He who is the Water of Life has nothing in Him that is susceptible to Satan's fiery darts of temptation. He did love us enough, though, to take our sins that we might be saved.

4. All men are sinners as a result of Adam's disobedience when he ate of the forbidden fruit. It wasn't the apple up the tree that caused sin, it was the *pair* on the ground! (Romans 5:12) We were shaped in iniquity and in sin did our mother conceive us (Psalm 51:5). Consequently, we have all sinned and come short of the glory of God and the wages of our sin is death (Romans 3:23; 6:23a). It is appointed unto man once to die and after that the judgment and if he dies in sin, hell awaits him (Hebrews 9:27; Matthew 10:28; Luke 16:16:22–24).

5. Jesus Christ is man's *only* hope of escaping a devil's hell. In eternity past He

was foreordained to be God's sacrificial Lamb for sin (Revelation 13:8b). When Satan brought sin into the world through Adam and Eve, Christ was the promised "Seed" to defeat him (Genesis 3:15). When he came into the world to save sinners, He came in the fulness of God's time, born of a woman to redeem those under the curse of sin (Galatians 4:4,5). God commended His love toward us in that while we were yet sinners Christ died for our sins, was buried and came forth from the grave to justify us, to redeem us from a devil's hell (Romans 5:6–8). All who believe on Him are saved from their sins and are given the right to become His child. They will not come into judgment and condemnation, but are passed from death unto life (John 1:12; 5:24). We are saved by God's grace through Christ and God's promise of eternal life is a gift which cannot be earned by our works (Ephesians 2:8,9).

Christ did not die for a certain elect, thus condemning the rest. He did not limit His blood sacrifice to just the elect with no sacrifice for the non-elect. He is the propitiation—atonings-sacrifice—for the sins of *every* sinner, the whole world (I John 1:2). That is why He loved the *whole world* and made it possible for *all* who believed on His only begotten Son would have eternal life (John 3:16). Jesus Christ is the Savior of all men, *especially those who believe* (I Timothy 2:3,4; 4:10). When the Lord died on the cross, He had you, me in mind. He paid a debt He didn't owe because we owed a debt that we couldn't pay. He spent a few years on this planet so that we could spend eternity with Him. Out of all the things Christ did for us while He was here in earth, we can ever be thankful that we did not have to be redeemed with corruptible things such as silver and gold or the traditions of men, but it was with His precious blood (I Peter 1:18,19).

6. Satan. He is the creator of sin. Originally named Lucifer, he sought to exalt himself above God, to be God himself. He was excommunicated from heaven and brought sin to the earth (I John 3:8a; Isaiah 14:12–14). He caused our first parents to sin in the Garden of Eden and from that time till this very moment and up to his final judgment, he still deals in sin. Satan is the arch enemy of the human race, and we need to study the Word of God to know best how to cope with his strategies. He has been in business with the human race for over 6,000 years and no one apart from the believer is a match for him.

> a. He is the "god of this age," whose one desire is to blind the minds of those who believe not, lest the light of the glorious Gospel of Christ, who is the image of God should shine unto them: (II Corinthians 4:4).
> b. He is the prince of the power of the air, the spirit that works in the children of disobedience (Ephesians 2:2).
> c. He is the prince of this world, seeking to keep world situations in his grasp, resulting in godlessness, immorality, wars and rumors of war, genocide, and hatred toward Christ and His followers (John 14:30). He causes suffering and death, attracts to evil, ensnares people by taking possession of them, inspires wicked thoughts and purposes, dissipates the truth, changes his demons into ministers of righteousness to deceive and changes himself into an angel of light to lead people down the wrong path.

Satan vs. Christians

Although Satan is not omnipotent (all powerful), he has access to all places, making the heavens his abode, but the earth the special place for his activities. Positionally, believers have been raised from the death of sin and have been raised up together to sit together in heavenly places in Christ Jesus where we are blessed with all spiritual blessings (Ephesians 2:5,6; 1:3). While still in our bodies we live and move and have our being on earth. Being both "in the heavenlies" and on earth, we are subject to the wiles (deceitful tactics) of Satan.

No believer has reached perfection, and there are times when one might give in to a temptation but thankfully God forgives when sin is *confessed* and *forsaken* (Proverbs 28:13; I John 1:9). Scripture offers many "weapons" for the believer to resist Satan and we are without excuse if we don't avail ourselves of His Word to overcome Satan like Christ did in the wilderness (Matthew 4:1–11). Christ was manifested that he might defeat Satan and in His fulfilling the first Messianic promise in the Bible by His crucifixion and resurrection, He defeated Satan and came forth from the grave victoriously with the "keys of hell and of death" (I John 3:8b; Revelation 1:5,18).

Christ's victory became our victory and we can "watch (be on the lookout for Satan) and pray that we enter not into temptation" (Matthew 26:41). Often people say "it is no sin to be tempted, only when we yield do we sin. However, often in flirting with temptation we are not abstaining from all appearances of evil, which leads to evil (sinful) thoughts (I Thessalonians 5:22). In Chapter Two under the heading of "Christ's Victory over Satan," it is revealed how Christ's victory is our victory and how we can be "more than conquerors through Christ who loves us:" (Romans 8:37).

7. There two Ordinances that have been given to local Churches to perform with believer's only—Baptism and the Lord's Supper, or Communion.

Baptism. Before one is baptized, there must be an admission that the candidate is truly saved—born again. Nowhere in Scripture do we read of infant baptism—it is for believers only. This we learn when the Eunuch asked Phillip what hindered him from being baptized after learning of Jesus and His death for Him as a sinner. Philip said, "if you believe with all your heart, you may," to which the Eunuch replied, "I believe that Jesus Christ is the Son of God." With this confession, Philip baptized him (Acts 8:35–39). Whenever a baptism took place and water is mentioned, the one baptized went down into enough water to come up out of it (Matthew 3:16; Acts 8:38,39).

Baptism by immersion sets *forth* in a visible symbol Christ's death, burial and resurrection, and also our death to the old life of sin, being raised to walk in a new way of life. No way can baptism be associated with one's being saved, for baptism at best is obedience to Christ's law or command to be baptized *after* learning what He taught in the Gospel and accepting Him as their Savior (Matthew 28: 19, 20). Submitting to this Ordinance does not put away the filth of the flesh (sin) but is an answer of a good conscience toward God for having trusted in Christ (I

Peter 3:21). It is a public testimony once and for all that one has joined ranks with the family of God. By all means infants should be dedicated publically to the Lord by *godly parents*.

The Lord's Supper or Communion. In the Upper Room where Christ gathered with His disciples, He instituted this Supper for believers. It is an Ordinance in which the bread and the fruit of the cup both symbolize His broken, suffering body and His precious shed blood in behalf of those who had sinned and come short of God's glory (Matthew 26:26–29). This Ordinance is done in remembrance of Christ's death, and as often as we observe it, we show forth His death 'till He comes again.

It is interesting to note that none of the references, either in the King James Version or the Catholic Bible, mention the world "wine." Jesus always used the word *cup* or *the fruit of the vine*, implying "new wine." In Bible times wine was referred to as "newly pressed grape juice" *or* "old wine," which was a "mocker, a strong drink", fermented, intoxicating (Proverbs 1:20). It is unreasonable to think for one moment that Christ would give to His disciples or expect us today to use an intoxicating beverage to commemorate the shedding of His blood as an acceptable sacrifice to God. The Roman Catholic Church in Mass uses fermented wine and say that the bread becomes the literal body of Christ and wine becomes the literal blood of Christ. Jesus used both *only* as *symbols*, nothing more.

8. A thrilling doctrinal truth is that of the "Blessed Hope," the glorious appearing of Christ *for* His family of believers, often referred to as the Rapture (Titus 2:13). This event is described in First Thessalonians 4:16,17. No one knows the day nor the hour of this event. After the catching up of His saints to be with Him forever, having become like Him, there is the "Judgment Seat of Christ" before which our works as His servants are judged by fire. If they have been God honoring, they will get a reward. If they were performed for self, we will see them burned up but thankfully, they will be saved (I Corinthians 3:9–15). Personally, I want all the rewards I can get, not for self, but to lay at the feet of Jesus and say, "Thank you, Lord, for saving my soul."

We will be in heaven with Christ for a period of seven years, which according to Daniel and the Book of Revelation, there will be a seven year tribulation period on earth and then Christ will return *with* His saints to rule and reign on the earth for 1,000 years in a kingdom of righteousness, at which time Satan will be bound in the bottomless pit (Revelation 20:1–4).

9. The Great White Throne Judgment. At the completion of the one thousand year reign of Christ the final judgment takes place. Satan meets his final doom and all whose names are not written in the Lamb's Book of Life are cast into the lake of fire, a place where the worm dies not and where there will be weeping and wailing and gnashing of teeth (Revelation 20:11,15; 21:8; Matthew 8:12; 13:42).

10. After the Great White Throne Judgment there will be a new heaven and a new earth. The old heaven shall pass away and the old earth will melt with fervent heat. A new heaven and a new earth will appear with a new Jerusalem. This new city is prepared for the redeemed of all ages to spend eternity with the Lord. What a day that will be and in a place wherein dwells righteousness (II Peter

3:10–13; Revelation 21:1,2). Paul tells us that "in the ages to come God will show us the exceeding riches of His kindness toward us through His Son, Jesus Christ" (Ephesians 2:7).

CONCLUSION

In this Chapter on "The Principle of Bible Study," we have sought to touch on the major subjects and doctrines for spiritual progress. We can never graduate from the "School of God" simply because His Word is *living*—alive.

It constantly gives the student light and direction. "Blessed is the man whose delight is in the Word of God and meditates in it day and night. He shall be like a tree planted by the rivers of water who brings forth his fruit in his season. His leaf also shall not wither, and whatsoever he does shall prosper" (Psalm 1:2,3). A worn Bible that's falling apart usually belongs to someone who isn't.

The writer of Psalm 119 left us a challenge and example to follow in our study and knowledge of the Bible. He used at least ten synonyms 168 times in referring to Scripture in 176 verses. What a student this man was. It is literally impossible for us to know enough Scripture but that is no excuse for not learning and knowing as much as we can. The late Dr. James M. Gray, president of the Moody Bible Institute was a master student of the Bible. Upon his deathbed a friend commended him for his knowledge of Scripture and his reply was, "I haven't even begun to scratch the surface." True, we will never "know it all" this side of heaven. If we could, there would be no room for faith. But if we practice Psalm 119:11 by hiding the word of God in our hearts,

> It will always be God's revelation to us.
> We will never lack authority.
> It will always give us boldness.
> We will never mislead a sinner.
> It will give us a better understanding of our salvation.
> It will reveal to us how much God loves us.
> It will never return unto us void.
> We will help to build up saints in the faith.
> It will be our Guide for faith and practice.
> It will give us standing with God.
> It will always keep us walking in fellowship with God.
> It takes the guesswork out of religion.
> Its message will always be timeless.

How to Study Your Bible[2]

Read and study the Bible *daily*, not as a newspaper but as a letter from your heavenly Father, as a letter from your eternal home. The Bible is the only book whose Author is always present whenever you read it. Move over and let God be seated with you to help you understand what is read.

When a cluster of heavenly fruit hangs within your grasp, gather it!

When a promise lies upon its pages as a blank check, cash it!

When a prayer is recorded, appropriate it and launch it as a feathered arrow from the bow of your desire!

When an example of holiness gleams before you, ask God to do as much for you!

When the truth of Christ is revealed in all its intrinsic splendor, entreat that His glory and beauty may ever irradiate the hemisphere of your life!

In closing let me offer the following suggestions—things that have been a challenge to perform as I live and move and have my being in His presence:

> —Let your utmost desire be to know and do the will of God for your life: John 7:17.
> —Make time for your daily Bible study and prayer time: Acts 3:1; 6:4.
> —When praying hold nothing back. Let every test and action be, "What would Jesus do?" When told, *do it*: I Peter 2:21.
> —Never forget that on a twenty-four hour basis we live in the presence of God because He lives in us. "The eyes of the Lord are in every place, beholding the good and the evil:" Proverbs 15:3. In conclusion—

The Bible Palace

"With the Holy Spirit as my Guide, I entered this wonderful Temple called the Bible. I entered the portico of Genesis, walked down through the Old Testament art gallery, where pictures of Enoch, Noah, Abraham, Moses, Joseph, Isaac, Jacob, and Daniel hung upon the wall. I passed into the music room of Psalms, where the Spirit swept the key-board of nature and brought forth a dirge-like wail of the weeping prophet Jeremiah to the grand, impassioned strain of Isaiah, until it seemed that every reed and pipe in God's great organ of nature responded to the tuneful harp of David, the sweet singer of Israel. I entered into the beautiful chapel of Ecclesiastes where the preacher's voice was heard and into the conservatory room of Sharon, and the Lily of the Valley's sweet-scented spices filled and perfumed my life. I entered the business office of Proverbs, then into the observatory room of the Prophets, where I saw telescopes of various sizes, some pointed to far-off events, but all concentrated upon the Bright and Morning Star which was to rise above the moon-lit hills of. Judea for our Salvation.

"I entered the audience-room of the King of kings, and caught a vision of His glory from Matthew, Mark, Luke and John. I then passed on into the field of the Acts of the Apostles where the Holy Spirit was forming the infant Church. Then into the correspondence room where sat Saints Paul, Peter, James, John and Jude penning their letters. I stepped into the throne room of Revelation where all towered in glittering peaks, and I got a vision of the King sitting upon His throne in all His glory, and I cried:

> "All hail the power of Jesus' name!
> Let angels prostrate fall;

Bring forth the royal diadem,
And crown Him Lord of all!"
Evangelist Billy Sunday

 Dear Father, as I grow in grace and knowledge of my Lord and Savior Jesus Christ through Your Word, may I, like the Psalmist be "stuck" (grasped by) Your Word to the degree that my one desire will be to make Christ known so that others might come to know Him whom to know is life eternal. In Jesus' name.   Amen. (Psalm 119:31,89; 138:2).

Chapter Two

THE PRINCIPLE OF THE SACRIFICE

Part One: Christ's Atoning Sacrifice

The "Principle of the Sacrifice" is the most important simply because it deals with the sacrifice of the Son of God in behalf of all who have sinned and come short of the glory of God, which includes *every* human being. It involves an obedient act on the part of the sinner to believe on the Lord Jesus Christ if he is ever to be saved from his sins (Rom 5:8; John 1:12).

When did this "Principle of the Sacrifice" begin? In the heart and mind of God it began in eternity past. Because God knows the end from the beginning, in His *foreknowledge* He saw that His crowning act of creation, man, would disobey Him and bring sin into the world. In His overall plan for His subjects who were originally created in His likeness and image, God provided a remedy for their sinfulness, His only Son—the blood of the Lamb who was slain from before the foundation of the world (Revelation 13:8).

From the standpoint of its application for lost mankind, it began in the Garden of Eden. True, the personal appearance of the Lamb of God had not taken place, but God started a workable rule that was acceptable until Christ would come upon the scene. God's order was a sacrifice which provided blood as an atonement for sin. We are told "it is the blood that makes atonement for the soul," and that "without the shedding of blood there is no remission or forgiveness" (Leviticus 17:11; Hebrews 9:22). This type of sacrifice is necessary for one's justification (Romans 5:5–9).

The story of our first parents, Adam and Eve, brings out the truth of the Principle of the Sacrifice. After their creation God gave them the privilege of eating of the fruit of every tree except one—His. They were warned if they ate of this "forbidden fruit" they would surely die, implying if they did not eat of His tree, they would remain alive (Genesis 2:16,17). As the story begins to unfold in Chapter Three, both of them disobeyed God, died spiritually, found themselves to be naked, covered themselves with fig leaves to hide from God. Their covering could be called "the fig-leaves of self-righteousness." When God located them in their hiding place, He used the method of interrogation to get to the *cause* of this broken fellowship. When He spoke to Adam, asking what he had done, he said his wife made him do it, blaming her (just like a man!). God abruptly broke conversation with Adam and turned to Eve. Learning from her husband how to shift the blame, she said the serpent (Satan) deceived (outwitted) me and I took a bite, blaming him. God abruptly broke conversation with her and arrived at the cause of Adam and Eve's sin, placing the blame squarely on the serpent by saying, "because *you* have done this" (vs. 14).

Satan was the originator of sin, for he sinned from the beginning (I John 3:8). Cast out of God's heaven for his sin of seeking to be like and above Him (Isaiah 14:12–15), here in the Garden he originates sin on earth. Since Adam and Eve were no match for Satan, God, a force greater than this enemy, had to strike at the *cause* of Adam's downfall. The punishment upon the serpent implied it stood erect, for it was cursed above all other animals and forced to crawl on its belly. Then in verse 15, God gave this enemy of mankind an ultimatum, saying, "I will put enmity between you and the woman and between your seed and her seed. It shall bruise your head and you shall bruise his [her Seed's] heel." This ultimatum to Satan is the first prophetic statement in Scripture concerning Christ's coming to atone for sin, His appearing as the "Seed of the woman" to redeem lost sinners (Galatians 4:4,5). The "bruising of Christ's heel" was not a matter of finalizing Him, but pictures His death at Calvary and also His resurrection, being made alive again. We will discuss Satan's bruising later.

Before God provided "coats of skin" for Adam and Eve, symbolizing a blood sacrifice as atonement for their sin to give them standing with Him again, God first had to settle a big score with the serpent. His great love not only provided salvation for them but did it while they were still in the Garden. He did not "throw them out" among thorns first but provided a blood sacrifice to restore fellowship before passing judgment. Both Abel and Noah offered blood sacrifices (Genesis 4:4; 8:20). When God told Abraham to offer his son Isaac as a sacrifice, he willingly made preparation in obedience to the Lord. When Isaac questioned where the lamb was for the offering, his father said, "My son, God will provide Himself— not *for* Himself—but *Himself* a lamb." This prefigured Christ's sacrifice and when the ram, caught in the thicket, became a substitute for Isaac, the ram became a type of Christ and Isaac, who was spared, became a picture of the sinner. Isaac was a type of Christ in that he was a "seed of promise." This was when Abraham "saw Christ's day and rejoiced in it" (Genesis 22:1–13 with John 8:56).

The Passover

As we approach this subject we are reminded of the truth we learned when God, who is a *greater* power than Satan, that old serpent, judged him before Adam and Eve were judged and redeemed. In the Book of Exodus we note that a powerful Pharaoh was responsible for Israel's slavery. God told Moses, since Israel was helpless to free herself under their enemy's power, what He would do to settle the score with Pharaoh (6:1). Israel is shown as a helpless sinner trying to free himself from sin. Pharaoh was a type of Satan who has sinners bound in his grip. In verse six, God said He would (1) bring Israel out from under the burdens of the Egyptians,

The Principle of the Sacrifice

(2) rid them of their bondage, and *then* (3) *redeem* them with an outstretched arm and with great judgments. God, a greater power than Pharaoh, was the only One who could deliver Israel from their helpless, hopeless situation, and the only One who could redeem these people. Notice the Divine order of deliverance:

1. The enemy has to be overpowered and defeated. We note this in Hitler's bondage of the Jews and the Holocaust during World War Two. It took a greater power than Hitler's to bring about defeat before any surviving Jews could be redeemed or set free. This was true in Adam's case before God provided "coats of skin." The *cause* of bondage had to be dealt with *first*. We usually say "get saved first and then our burdens will be rolled away," or dealt with. God must deal with the cause of our bondage first before He can turn and set us free. We will notice this when we come to Christ's sacrifice in our behalf.

2. God used judgment with Pharaoh and the Egyptians like He used judgment with the serpent in the Garden. From Exodus 7:1–11:10 we notice the plagues or judgment that came upon these people. God saw to it in a miraculous way that Israel escaped these plagues. Beginning with Exodus 11:1–12:36, God brought to pass the tenth and final judgment—that of the firstborn throughout the land dying, including Israel's. Israel, however, was given an out. God first instituted the Passover—the blood of lambs being sprinkled upon the door posts and at the top of the doors. All inside the house when the death angel passed over would be spared. Death would strike where no blood was applied. A power greater than the enemy had to strike in judgment and bring defeat if no blood was applied to a door post, no matter whose house it was, including Pharaoh's.

For Israel to be free from her bondage and make their exodus from the land of bondage, she must apply blood, and she did. When the firstborn of Egypt died because no blood was applied, this judgment forced Pharaoh to let the Israelites "pack their bags and take off!"

The Passover became the first of Israel's annual Feasts and is called both the Feast of the Passover and Feast of Unleavened Bread. It also started the dating of Israel's years, or a period of beginning, which signifies that a person doesn't begin to live for God until he has been cleansed by the blood of the Lamb and is born again.

The root meaning of the Passover is found in the word propitiation, which means a "covering." When the Lord came in judgment upon Egypt, when He saw the blood sprinkled on the doorposts that house was covered by those who exercised faith in His commandment. As the death angel passes by, the Lord's wrath was withheld and the Israelites were given deliverance. This ties in with the sprinkling of Christ's blood who has become our Passover for us in this age of grace (Galatians 1:4; I Corinthians 5:7). In the giving of the orders to sprinkle the blood, we notice it was to be on the two side posts and the upper post of the door. Why was no blood to be sprinkled on the threshold? "Of how much sorer punishment will one deserve who tramples under foot the Son of God and regards His blood of the covenant as unclean, insulting the spirit of grace." To trample under foot His blood will cause one to fall into the hands of an angry God (Hebrews 10:29–31).

After the Passover, Israel left Goshen in Egypt after many years of bondage.

Beginning their wilderness journey to the Promised Land, God made provision for them to cross the Red Sea dry-shod and led them southward to Mt. Sinai (Genesis 12;39–19:25). Having previously stated that man does evil things due to a natural mind—things the Principle mentions in the Ten Commandments, these laws spell out what sin is, putting it down in "black and white" for man to know how God sees sin. Man already had the "law written in his heart," and God is letting him know that these things are wrong and if committed, atonement must be made by blood for their forgiveness. These commandments are not *suggestions* that give permission to or not to but a *law* that says unless obeyed they are broken. To obey them means we please the heart of God. Israel as a nation and mankind in general needed such laws to constantly remind them that only a blood sacrifice would avail for them when sin was committed. There are no loopholes in God's commandments.

Not only did God give Moses the Ten Commandments on Mt. Sinai, He gave a pattern for the Tabernacle, which served as a shadow or type of Christ and His sacrificial offering. Due to Israel's sin of idolatry at Mount Sinai, the Tribe of Levi took a stand with Moses and were later included in the Levitical priesthood (Exodus 32:26). Two feasts celebrated the "Principle of the Sacrifice," the Passover, which has already been discussed, and the-

Day of Atonement

On this day the High priest, wearing a single robe, entered the Holy of Holies in the Tabernacle where he sprinkled the blood of two sacrificial animals on the Altar. One was offered for his sins and the other was offered for the people of the nation. This day was unique because of other sin offerings, one of which was for sins of ignorance or of any committed unintentionally. In such cases the person was to bring a "Guilt Offering" and make a blood sacrifice for atonement. As the priest laid his hands on a living goat and confessed the sin or sins, this symbolized God's forgiveness and the goat was driven into the wilderness as a scapegoat (Leviticus 4:2–5; 16:10). To make these offerings effective faith always had to be predominant in each sacrifice. When God's people, through godly sorrow, obeyed God in this observance, His mercy provided forgiveness, thus challenging them to continue walking in obedience.

These holy days, "Feast of the Passover" and the "Day of Atonement," serve as a shadow or type to help the Israelites realize that when sin comes between them and God, there must be a confession and a blood sacrifice to have them blotted out. In their obedience, making amends with God, it helped prepare them to better understand that in the coming of Messiah, He was coming to redeem them from the curse of the law and bring them under a new covenant (Galatians 4:4,5; Hebrews 8:7–12).

After the Passover was instituted, Israel left Egypt. At Mount Sinai God gave Moses the Ten Commandments. The Principle was added because of sin, to let Israel know that God demanded obedience for His approval and this law was to be met until the *Seed* should come (Galatians 3:19). It was to serve as a "schoolmaster" to lead them to the coming Messiah (Galatians 3:24). Israel needed to know

The Principle of the Sacrifice 19

that if God's law was broken it was a sin on her part and by observing the Passover, they were looking to *Christ, the Passover* for forgiveness (I Corinthians 5:7b)

Going back to the Garden of Eden event in which Adam and Eve disobeyed God, this started the "Conflict of the Ages" between God and Satan. God uses people in His service and Satan, the great Imitator, does likewise. From Eden to the end of Old Testament period, Satan did all he could to thwart God from providing a "Seed" who would ultimately defeat him and offer a blood sacrifice that would provide a redemption that offers forgiveness and liberates all in his power.

It appeared God was defeated when Cain killed Abel but He raised up Seth. Although there were some like Seth and Enoch who walked with God, Satan was so victorious in causing man to become wicked to the point every imagination of the thoughts of his heart was evil continually (Genesis 6:5). God stepped in, sending a universal flood, saving only eight humans, Noah and his family (Genesis 6–8).

With the beginning of a new race, it wasn't long until Satan led people to reach heaven *their* way in building the Tower of Babel. God simply came down, confused their tongues and scattered them as separate nations (Genesis 11). Satan continued his dirty work such as causing people to dig deeper into sin by worshiping Baal, which he thought would keep anyone from bearing God's "Seed." God then called Abram (Abraham) to become the head of His nation and designated one from the Tribe of Judah to be that *Seed*.

From this point on Satan worked overtime to drag Israel so low in sin that no one would qualify to be the "Seed." On one occasion he almost succeeded. Queen Athaliah sought to murder all the males in this lineage, but a nurse hid the babe Joash, the last surviving member of the "Seed Royal." At the age of seven he was anointed king and the queen was slain (II Kings 11:1–16). In spite of all that Satan did throughout Israel's Old Testament history, God overruled. He is Omniscient—all knowing—and since Satan doesn't know it all, God is always one step ahead of him. There was a small group of faithful believers called the "remnant" and God through them preserved the lineage through whom Messiah would come (Isaiah 1:9).

The Time of the "Seed's" Arrival

God always moves in mysterious ways His wonders to perform. After His long period of silence, He begins to fulfill prophecy by announcing the birth of Christ's forerunner, John the Baptist (Luke 1;13,76,77). He then sent an angel to a young virgin named Mary to tell her she was chosen by God to bear the long awaited promised "Seed" of the woman (Luke 1:26–38). Joseph, who was engaged to her, was troubled and concerned about her pregnancy, but an angel appeared unto him. He was informed that her conception was by the Holy Spirit, and that her baby would be named Jesus, who would save His people from their sins (Matthew 1:18–25). Luke gives us an account of His birth in Bethlehem (2:1–14).

The Scripture is silent where Mary and Joseph took Jesus after he was seen by the shepherds in a manger. It is quite possible they went to the house of Mary's cousin, Elizabeth. At the age of eight days Jesus was circumcised and upon the completion of Mary's forty days of purification, the family went to the Temple in Jerusalem (Leviticus 12:2–6). There they were recognized by Simeon and Anna, the prophetess, both students of the Scriptures who looked for the coming Messiah. Upon seeing Jesus, Simeon took the babe Jesus in his arms and exclaimed, "now my eyes have seen God's *salvation.*" Anna recognized him as *redemption.* After visiting the Temple according to the law, they left Jerusalem, returned to Joseph's home in Nazareth and settled there (Luke 2:21–39).

A question arises at this point. When the Wise Men followed the star that appeared to them in the East, they met with Herod in Jerusalem and asked, "Where is He who is born King of the Jews?" When Herod learned He was born in Bethlehem, he asked them what time the star appeared. When told, by this time Jesus must have been between one and two years old because Herod told the Wise Men to go search for the *young child.* As these men left, the star reappeared and led them to the house where the young child was. *Were they led to Bethlehem?* All the Christmas manger scenes say "yes." They were led to Nazareth where the family went after visiting the Temple when Jesus was forty days old (Luke 2:39 with Matthew 2:1–13).

Because the Wise Men did not return to Jerusalem at Herod's request to tell him they had seen the young child, Satan once again sought to slay Jesus through Herod's decree that all males two years and under would be slaughtered. This would have included the "Promised Seed" of Genesis 3:15. Joseph was warned to take his wife and Jesus to Egypt for protection until Herod died. Once again Satan's attempt to rid the world of God's promise of Messiah failed (Matthew 2:13–23).

Several lessons can be learned from these Wise Men.

1. They did not give up on their long trek from the East to Jerusalem, traveling several hundreds of miles, no doubt by camel.
2. They continued to follow the provision God gave, the "Bright and Morning Star," to come to find The Kings of the Jews, Jesus.
3. When they did find the young child, Jesus, they worshiped *Him*, not Mary, not Joseph, but *Jesus* (Matthew 2:lla).
4. Having brought gifts for the King, they gave them to *Him only*. Some have suggested that the gift of *incense* was to Jesus as their God, *gold* was to Him as their King and *Myrrh* was in relation to His sufferings and death for the sins of the world (Matthew 2:11a). They gave their best.
5. When they left the family in Nazareth, they were warned by God not to go back and report to Herod where Jesus was. They went home *another way*. When one recognizes and accepts Jesus as Savior, they do not go back the old "way." As a new creation, old things begin to pass away, all things become new and they follow Christ as *the Way* (II Corinthians 5:17; John 14:6).

When Jesus was twelve years old He was taken by his parents to Jerusalem for the Passover. Upon completion, he remained behind and was later found in the

The Principle of the Sacrifice

Temple confounding the Rabbis with His knowledge of the Scriptures. When found and questioned by his mother about not returning home with them, He replied, "I must be about My Father's business" (Luke 3:41–49). "Being about His Father's business" is translated "going about to do My Father's Will." And what was His Father's Will for Him? To be God's "Principle of the Sacrifice" in shedding His blood to make atonement for all mankind. He came to do God's will—born to die, to finish the work God sent Him to do, to fulfill all types and shadows of the blood sacrifices of the Old Testament, to do away with the Old Covenant and establish the New Covenant by becoming God's sacrifice in the offering of Himself *once and for all*. His blood sacrifice would never have to be repeated like those of the Old Testament which had to be performed over and over, year after year, by the Levitical Priesthood (Hebrews 1:3; 10:7–10).

Christ's next encounter with Satan was in the "wilderness of temptation" after His Baptism. Satan could not get Christ to bow down and worship him, so for a season Satan left Him. But as Christ started His earthly ministry, He preached in the city of Nazareth that "This is the acceptable year for the Anointed One to preach the Gospel, to heal the brokenhearted, give sight to the blind, giving deliverance to captives and set people at liberty. Giving deliverance to captives and setting free had to do with His coming to offer a blood sacrifice to set sinners free from the bondage of their sin and the wrath of God. The Jewish religious leaders were filled with wrath for His claiming to be the "Fulfiller" of Scripture and sought to kill Him, but Satan lost this battle and Jesus escaped unharmed (Luke 4:18–30).

Why were the Jews so vehement in their attitude toward Jesus? Retracing our steps back to the period during the 400 silent years, a Greek general, Antiochus Epiphanes, sought to force Grecian religion and culture on the Jews, refusing to allow them to circumcise their sons and by offering a pig on the Temple altar. To the Jews, this was an unpardonable sin. Going to war with this general and his army (about 165 B.C.), the Jews won and under the leadership of the Maccabeans, Jewish rule was reinstated over their territory.

In being released from Grecian tyranny, the Maccabeans violated the Levitical priesthood order, established their own, and became political leaders instead of spiritual. They slaughtered the true (fundamental) priests to propagate their false, traditional beliefs, but some priests managed to escape. They fled to Qumran near the Dead Sea, made copies of the Scriptures, and later hid the now famous Dead Sea Scrolls in nearby caves. In 63 B.C. the Romans conquered the land, changed some Jewish laws, but from the religious standpoint, the Jews became all the more political and perverted.

By the time of Christ's day, these Jewish leaders were so ungodly the position of the high priest was purchased through bribery and the Scriptures had become null and void, having absolutely no meaning to them. To these Jewish leaders—the Pharisees, Scribes, and Sadducees, Christ was a heretic, a false prophet, a blasphemer, not the true Messiah (*Seed*) of the Torah (the five Books of Moses), the Psalms, and the Prophets. They had been so blinded by their traditions that no matter where He went or what He preached, they often sought ways to rid themselves of Him.

As the "Promised Seed" to a lost and dying world, and as this "Seed" being the promised Messiah to the descendants of father Abraham, Jesus came unto His own and His own received Him not. Having been blinded by their traditions, the priests and Pharisees refused to let the people believe anything their Scriptures taught. But the Lord, all through His earthly ministry, sought to let both Jew and Gentile know the purpose of His coming according to the prophet, Daniel, the One who would be the sacrifice to "finish the transgression," to put away sin and to make reconciliation for iniquity and to bring in everlasting righteousness" (9:24). The Scriptures made known to them that this Messiah, the "King of the Jews.[3]

1. Was born to save sinners: Matthew 1:21; I Timothy 1:15
2. Was born to die, to give His life a ransom for many: Matthew 20:28
3. Came to seek and save the lost: Luke 19:10
4. Must suffer at the hands of the religious leaders, be killed and raised the third day: Matthew 16:21
5. Came to be the "Seed" of the woman to defeat Satan: Galatians 4:4,5
6. Must be lifted up on a Cross to die for sinners so that those who believe in Him might not perish but have everlasting life: John 3:14–17
7. Came to give us life and to have it more abundantly: John 10:10
8. Came to be our "Burden Bearer" and give us rest: Matthew 11:28–30
9. Came to offer fallen man the only Hope of a future home (house) in heaven: John 14:1–3

There are many other verses in which we find the purpose of Christ's coming, but the tragedy in the New Testament is the same as we find in the Old—the Jews were dead set in refusing to believe and accept what God had commanded them to do for atonement for their soul's salvation. Christ was fought at every turn, his life was threatened often to be killed, but God always brought Him through unscathed for His time had not yet come as He continued His earthly ministry.

As we approach the last week of Jesus' earthly ministry, He begins to focus primarily on the "Day of Atonement," the time He will fulfill His Father's will in His crucifixion. At the institution of the "Lord's Supper" it is made known who will betray Him, namely Judas. This betrayer goes to the Jews who are determined to put Christ to death, and is paid thirty pieces of silver to betray Him into the hands of the Priests and their officers. After having prayer in the Garden of Gethsemane, when He submits totally to God's will, Judas comes with the Jews and Roman soldiers to arrest Him after planting the betrayal kiss upon Jesus. He is taken to Annas' house where a mock trial is held. After being insulted, He is then taken to the house of the high priest, Caiaphas, for another mock trial. The Jews wanted to kill him then but because it was a feast day they didn't. After finding Him guilty of false charges of blasphemy, which was punishable by death, He was taken to Pilate because only Rome could sentence someone to die.

We are all familiar with the trial before Pilate. This Roman governor found

The Principle of the Sacrifice 23

Him innocent on three occasions, but giving in to the demands of the Jews, he permitted Christ to be scourged and sentenced Him to death by crucifixion. At Calvary the spikes were driven into His hands and feet, and after six agonizing hours, He said "It is finished." The "Principle of the Sacrifice," which was established in the Garden of Eden, was culminated in this act of atonement by Jesus Christ. We are told by the Apostle Paul that "when we were yet without strength, in due time Christ died for the ungodly. that God commended His love toward us in that, while we were sinners, Christ died for us" (Romans 5:6–8).

The offerings in Old Testament days were by the blood of lambs and goats but how much more shall the blood of Christ, who through the eternal Spirit offered Himself without spot to God, purge your conscience from dead works to serve the living God [by faith] (Hebrews 9:14). At Calvary "Jesus paid it all, all to Him I owe."

Christ's Victory over Satan

When Christ finished the will of God in being offered *once and for all*, when by *Himself* He purged our sins, he went through everything that a lost sinner would have to go through if he died in his sins—in unbelief, for the wages of sin is death (Romans 6:23a; Hebrews 1:3; 10:10). He would have to go to a Christless eternity just like the rich man who died and went to hell (Luke 16:23). This condition of lost man necessitated Christ to taste death for every man (Hebrews 2:9). It also necessitated Christ, during the time His body was in the grave for three days and three nights to descend into hell. There, as a "town crier," he informed the "spirits in prison" of His suffering for their sins. Here He "bruised the head of the serpent," that old serpent the devil, and gained complete victory (I Peter 3:18,19). Having fulfilled the first Messianic promise in the Bible, He came forth from the grave alive for evermore with the keys of hell and of death (Revelation 1:18). He is our *Principle of the Sacrifice*. To disobey the law of believing on Him and receiving Him as your own personal Savior is to break it and die in unbelief (John 3:18,36).

The victory Christ wrought at Calvary over Satan belongs to every born again believer. When the seventy returned from their ministry they remarked to Jesus they had victory over Satan's henchmen. To Jesus, this was no surprise since He had given them "power" over all the "power" of His enemy (Luke 10:17–19). The word *power* is used twice but in the Greek each has a different meaning. Satan's "power" is "dunamis," from which we get the word "dynamite." The other Greek word "power" is "exousia," meaning *authority*. When General McArthur brought about victory over the Japanese in World War II, as powerful as our enemy was, the authority back of McArthur brought about their surrender. Faith in Christ's victory assures us that we have a victory that can overcome the world (I John 1:4,5). We can submit ourselves to God, resist the devil, and he will flee from us (James 4:7). We have been given the whole armor of God to stand against the wiles (deceits) of Satan (Ephesians 6:10–18). We have the promise that what ever temptation comes our way, God is faithful who will not permit us to face a temptation that we cannot bear, but He will with any temptation help us to hold our own (I Corinthians 10:13). And, to add insult to Satan's injury, we *are* more than conquerors—not *shall be*, but *are* more than conquerors through Christ who loves us (Romans 8:37). We *have* God's authority and power over Satan.

CONCLUSION

Our minds will never be able to comprehend the full meaning of *atonement* this side of glory. Because of God's "Principle of the Sacrifice," Christ Himself, we have been made one in Him, we have been given a covering that gives us standing with God Himself, all because Christ by Himself has purged, cleansed and purified us. God presents Him to us as a sacrifice of atonement through faith in His blood. He did this to demonstrate His justice in blotting out our past sins and to declare us righteous (Romans 3:25).

The work of redemption in behalf of every sinner is now complete—finished. No other sacrifice is needed—no other one will save. What Christ did was *once and for all* in His death, burial and resurrection. After this momentous event, Christ spent forty days on earth before going back to be with His Father, to be seated on the right hand of His Majesty on high in heaven. Now as our Great High Priest, He is accomplishing His "Unfinished Ministry," that of "Saving all who come unto God by Him, seeing that He ever lives to make intercession for them" (Hebrews 1:3; 7:25).

Being the Savior of the world, especially of those who believe in Him, He is right now praying for the lost to come unto God by Him, and is also, as our Great High Priest, the Intercessor, praying for believers (I Timothy 2:5; 4:10b). We have learned in this chapter of the "Principle of the Sacrifice," that salvation is not in a Church, a ritual, baptism, good works, etc. It is impossible for someone to save another, "for no man can by any means redeem his brother nor give to God a ransom for him" (Psalm 49:7). God's salvation is in a *Person*, the Lord Jesus Christ, "for there is none other Name under heaven given among men whereby we must be saved" (Acts 4:12). *He is the only Way* (John 14:6).

If you are a recipient of God's "so great salvation." having become a child of the King by permitting Christ to become your personal Savior, bow your heart right now and thank God that His great love for you began in eternity past when the Lamb was slain for your sins (Revelation 13: 8b).

> Christ does not save men by His life,
> Though that was holy, sinless and pure; Nor even by His tender love,
> Though that forever shall endure.
> He does not save them by His Words
> Though they shall never pass away; Nor by His vast creative power
> That holds the elements in sway.
> He does not save them by His works, Though He is ever doing good;
> The awful need was greater still,
> It took His death, His cross, His blood[4]

The Principle of the Sacrifice

Part II: The Believer's Living Sacrifice

Considering the tremendous price Christ paid in the "Principle of the Sacrifice" for sin there is a sacrifice each child of His must offer unto Him. We are admonished "by the mercies of God to present our bodies a living sacrifice, holy, acceptable unto Him, which is our reasonable service (Romans 12:1). Having been bought with a price and are no longer servants of man or sin, all that we are and have—nothing withheld—belongs to God and Christ must have first place in our lives (I Corinthians 7:23; Romans 6:17,18).

After Paul tells us the need to sacrifice our bodies as a *living* sacrifice unto God, he then tells us *why* we should do this. We "must not be conformed to this world, but be transformed [completely changed] by the renewing of our minds that we may prove what the will of God is, that which is good and acceptable and perfect" (Romans 12:2). Accepting Christ as our Savior, we have become new creatures in Christ, with old things passing away and all things becoming new (II Corinthians 5:17). As new creatures, Paul outlines in Romans 12:3–21 God's requirements for our performing His perfect will. Having Christ's mind we are to "cast down imaginations and every high thing that exalts itself against the knowledge of God, and bring into captivity every thought [in our minds] to the obedience of Christ and have in readiness to punish all disobedience, by fulfilling our obedience to the "Principle of our Living Sacrifice" (I Corinthians 2:16; II Corinthians 10:5,6). What a joy it is then when be begin to grow in grace and knowledge of our Lord and Savior Jesus Christ (II Peter 3:15).

A Prayer Thought

> Dear Lord, help me to never forget that I was once purged from my old sins. Encourage me as Your "Living Sacrifice" to share with those who have never tasted and found that You are good, the one Sacrifice of Your dear Son for the sins of the world. Amen. (Psalm 34:8; I Timothy 1:15,16)

Chapter Three

THE PRINCIPLE OF THE PRIESTHOOD

When the *Principle of the Sacrifice* was instituted in the Garden of Eden, the blood sacrifice became valid for those who by faith and obedience had applied to themselves God's "coats of skin," which brought them nigh God (Genesis 3:21 with Ephesians 2:13). Only as we are obedient to this Principle can God give us a "covering" whereby our sins are forgiven and our past is blotted out.

Upon our acceptance of Christ, we notice the second Principle which is applicable, the "Principle of the Priesthood." Defining *priest* or *priesthood*, the word simply means to intercede—to go to God in behalf of either self and/or others. Adam, having sinned but cleansed by a blood sacrifice, outside the Garden he knew it was his responsibility to continue that practice, no doubt at an altar, and intercede for his wife and family. The fact that Cain and Abel came at the proper time to offer their sacrifice shows that Adam had become faithful in bringing up his children in the things of the Lord. Abel was an obedient child, but Cain was not (Genesis 4:1–7).

No doubt as sons and daughters of Adam grew and through marriage multiplied, some of the husbands, as the head of the home, built an altar and offered sacrifices for himself and his family. We can be assured men like Seth and Enoch, who walked with God, did likewise, thereby becoming the family priest. This pattern was followed closely by Noah when he made his exit from the ark. He built an altar and offered sacrifices for himself and his family, interceding for them as the priest. God not only blessed him for this sweet smelling sacrifice but blessed his whole family as well (Genesis 8:20–9:1).

When Abraham was called of God from Ur of the Chaldees to go to the land of Canaan, he built an altar at Shechem for himself and his kinsmen, and then journeying further south, he also built an altar at Bethel (Genesis 12:1–9). After a brief visit to Egypt due to a famine, he returned "unto the place of the altar, which he had made there at the first, and there called upon the name of the Lord" in behalf of self and those with him (Genesis 13:1–4). When Abraham and Lot came to the parting of the way due to their herdsmen not getting along, Lot chose the fertile plains near Sodom, and Abraham was content with what was left. But God turns the barren-looking land into a universal blessing and gives him and his seed the whole of the Promised Land. Abraham calls for a celebration and builds an altar unto God in appreciation for His goodness in honoring his faith (Genesis 13:5–18).

As Abraham was blessed by God, Isaac, a seed of promise, was given. We are familiar with God's request of Abraham to offer Isaac as a sacrifice. An altar was built but God gave a substitute, a ram, to be offered instead of his son (Genesis 22:1–14). As Abraham interceded for God to provide Himself the sacrifice, He saw Christ's day and rejoiced in it (John 8:56). We notice that Isaac and Jacob also practiced this same law in establishing altars (Genesis 26:24,25; 31:54).

As we come up to the days of Moses, we notice that his father in-law was a priest (Exodus 3:1). So far we conclude that these incidents seem to indicate that the head of each family was a family priest. With Israel "organized," having established the Passover, they had this recognition by God. Three months after they arrived at Mt. Sinai, here the Lord told Israel that if they would obey His voice and keep His covenant, He would make them His peculiar (special) people and they would be unto Him a *kingdom of priests* (Exodus 19:1–6). God's children, as a nation or kingdom, was given the privilege of becoming a people who would go to God not only in behalf of their own individual selves, but if obedient, they would be used by God to let others know they were a people called by His name and so win them to the Lord (Deuteronomy 28:9,10). They would have charge of the various sacrifices which were to be offered—each family head being responsible to God in every detail of His requirements of them.

In making this promise to the children of Israel, God told Moses He would come in a thick cloud and that the people would hear Him when He spoke with him (vs. 9). He told Moses to get the people clean (consecrated) and that He would come down the third day. On that day there were great thunders and lightenings and a thick cloud (vss. 10,11, 16–25). Then God *spoke* the Ten Commandments to the people (Exodus 20:1–17). When the people saw the lightning, smoke, etc., they were afraid and said they did not want God to speak to them, but requested that Moses do the talking (vss. 18,19).

What a privilege for them to have had God speak to them personally since He said if they obeyed Him they would be a *kingdom of priests*, people who could talk to God personally and God could speak to them. They did not want God to speak to them for fear they would die, so they requested that Moses be their "priest" or intercessor. This was their first act of disobedience.

God did speak much to Moses, which he had to write down, and then God called Moses to go up on Mt. Sinai to receive the tablets of stone on which He had written the Ten Commandments (Exodus 24:9–18). God also gave Moses instructions for the building of the Tabernacle, which included all the furniture, vessels, altars, etc., to be placed in it (25:3–26:19).

The Priesthood

We mentioned in the previous Chapter that God, who knows the end from the beginning, provided the "slain Lamb" before the foundation of the world for man who would sin. In seeking to make of the Israelites a "kingdom of priests" if they

The Principle of the Priesthood 29

obeyed Him, He knew they would disobey, would not want Him to speak to them, so He instituted the "Principle of the Priesthood." Aaron was chosen to be the high priest and his sons were to minister in the office of the priests. In Exodus 28:1 through 31:17 the duties, type of wearing apparel, sacrifices, food for the priests, etc., were listed. Sabbath duties were also given. God then gave Moses the two tables of stone containing the Ten Commandments and he started down the mountain to meet with the people in the valley (Exodus 31:18).

Due to Moses' lengthy absence, the people thought he had abandoned them so they got Aaron to make the "golden calf" and worshiped it. This is disobedience number two (32:1–6). Moses had been informed the people were defiling themselves and when he saw first-hand their sin and debauchery, he threw down the stone tables and broke them. God wanted to consume them and make a nation from Moses, but he pled with God not to destroy them. He took the golden calf, ground it to powder, put it in water and made the people drink it. See Exodus 32:7–19; 34:1–4,29–35. How Aaron wriggled out of the blame is a mystery to me, but that's something he will have to give an account for to the Lord

When Moses saw the people were dancing naked, he cried out, "Who is on the Lord's side?" All the sons of Levi gathered together with him, and from this Tribe came the "Levitical Priesthood" (Exodus 32:5, 26). Aaron, the High priest, made atonement once a year for the sins of Israel in the Holy of Holies, and it was in the Tabernacle that God dwelt among His people (Exodus 25:8).

Types or Shadows of Christ and Believers

1. Mt. Sinai has often been said to be a type of the Principle, for here God gave the Ten Commandments. It is a type of the Principle, but on this mountain God gave the pattern (instructions) for the building of the Tabernacle, which is a type of Christ, thus making Mt. Sinai a type of both Principle and Grace.

2. Aaron, the high priest, is a type of Christ.[5]

   a. He was called of God: Hebrews 5:4.
   b. He made the proper sacrifice for sin: Leviticus 16:11,15.
   c. He was the mediator between God and man: I Timothy 2:5.
   d. He was anointed: Leviticus 8:12 with Acts 10:38.

3. Aaron's sons, a type of believers.[6]

   a. We are sons of the High Priest, Jesus Christ: John 1:12.
   b. We have the same calling, as priests: Revelation 1:5,6.
   c. We are God's servants: Romans 6:18.
   d. We have been anointed: Leviticus with I John 2:27.
   e. We are under the same authority: John 15:14.

In the Tabernacle, which was God's dwelling place, the priests performed all the sacrifices and acts of worship commanded by the Principle. It was the responsibility of the priests to set the example of dedication and true worship to God, to intercede in their behalf, to read the Scriptures to the people, do everything God commanded to help His people be the shining example He called them to be.

As we follow Israel's history, one of her biggest problems was the failure of priests to set the example God called them to be. Prophets were placed on the scene to pronounce God's judgment upon priests and people alike for their failure to observe the rituals of the Tabernacle (and Temple). Too often these prophets were persecuted, stoned, banished, and even slain. Failure on the part of the priests and people resulted in their transgressing very much by following all the abominations of the heathen nations and polluting the house of the Lord which He had hallowed (II Chronicles 36:14).

To add insult to injury, we noticed in the previous Chapter that when the Maccabeans won their freedom from the Greek General, Antiochus, that when they assumed the role of the priesthood which belonged to the descendants of the sons of Aaron and the Tribe of Levi. Thus the *Principle of the Priesthood*, as ordained by God in the Old Testament, came to an end and was of no value even during the lifetime of Christ.

The New Testament Principle of the Priesthood

As we examine the priesthood in the Gospel accounts and the Book of Acts, there were false priests, but they controlled the Jewish people as whole. However, in our approach to the Epistles, we see the Old Testament system, with its sacrifices and priesthood, is set aside in Christ. With His one sacrifice in accomplishing our salvation, He has been ordained as our High Priest after the order of Melehizedek, the king and priest of Salem (Hebrews 5:5,6). Why this change from the Levitical priesthood?

The Bible doesn't give us much information about this "king and priest of Salem," a city identified with Jerusalem. He is mentioned about 500 years prior to the institution of the Levitical priesthood. His name means "king of righteousness." After Abraham won victory over five kings, Melchizedek went out to meet him and presented him with bread and wine in the name of "God most high, possessor of heaven and earth." Abraham gave him tithes of all he possessed. Some scholars are of the opinion that this priest is what is called a *"Theophany,"* an appearance of Christ in human form in Old Testament days. Another example is found in Joshua in reference to the "Captain of the Lord's host" (5:13–15).

To answer the question why the priesthood changed from the Levitical to after the order of Melchizedek, Melchizedek was without beginning of days or end of life, which is a type of the Son of God, and thus has a timeless priestly authority (Hebrews 7:1–3). The Levitical priesthood recognized that Aaron was in the lineage of Abraham, but Abraham recognized Meichizedek as a priest, showing that God had ordained *an eternal* priesthood for the One who was to take up Melchizedek's role, while the Aaronic priesthood was destined to come to an end (Hebrews 7:4–28). Also interesting symbolically is Melchizedek offering to Abraham "bread and wine" (fruit of the cup), which speaks of Christ's death (Mark

The Principle of the Priesthood

14:22–25). In Abraham's giving Melchizedek "tithes of all" (Genesis 14:18–20), this could speak to us about examining ourselves before we take communion as to whether we have given to God what rightly belongs to Him. One other thing we should keep in mind is that Christ, our High Priest, who ever lives to make intercession for us, is of the Tribe of Judah, not Levi (Revelation 5:5; Hebrews 7:25).

A most precious truth in Christ's coming to be our High Priest is that we, as believers, have personal access to Him. No where in the Bible are we instructed to go to Him through His mother or through an earthly person who was ordained as a priest. Through the new and living way made possible by Christ, we have personal access to God through our Great High Priest. It is not a matter of our entering into God's presence, we are already there as His child. But we are invoked to "come boldly before His throne of grace to obtain mercy and find grace to help in our time of need" (Hebrews 10:19,20; 4:14–16). Only the high priest in Old Testament days could enter the Holy of Holies, and that only once a year, but under the New Testament "Principle of the Sacrifice," any believer, any time, can come boldly to meet with God and His Son.

Every believer is a priest—a member of the *holy priesthood*, a *royal priesthood*. God desired the children of Israel to be a kingdom of priests, a peculiar people, an holy nation—His chosen people. In disobedience, the people failed, but now with Christ as our High Priest, every born again believer is all that God wanted Israel to be—a "chosen generation, a royal priesthood, a holy nation, and a peculiar people" (I Peter 2:9a). The Apostle John emphasized this truth that all who had been washed from their sins in the blood of Christ *are* His royal priests (Revelation 1:5,6; 5:10).

Positionally, we *are* God's royal priesthood. We put it into practice by "showing forth the praises of Him who has called us out of darkness into His marvelous light" (I Peter 2: 9b). This is how we obey the New Testament "Principle of the Priesthood." *It must be put into practice*.

There are several ways we can "show and tell" others what great things God has done for us. As a priest, we can offer "spiritual sacrifices" unto the Lord. As priests, our body is God's Temple on earth, the Temple in which the Triune God dwells—God the Father (II Corinthians 6:16), God the Son (Colossians 1:27), and God the Holy Spirit (I Corinthians 3:16). What are some "spiritual sacrifices" we can offer?"

1. Our bodies: Romans 12:1; 6:19,20
2. Our *thanksgiving*, declaring the works of God with rejoicing: Psalm 107:22 with I Thessalonians 5:18.
3. Our *praise* to the One who is worthy, Jesus, our Great High Priest: Jeremiah 33:11; Psalm 18:3; Hebrews 13:15.
4. A *sweet smelling* savor as we walk in love for Christ and before one another, and for our service in helping to supply the needs of others: Ephesians 5:2 with Philippians 4:18. There is no set time for these sacrifices. Our obligation as priests is to be faithful in offering them continually.

SUMMARY

It is evident from the Book of Hebrews that the old Levitical priesthood under Aaron and the Tribe of Levi is a thing of the past. The new priesthood is in Christ and those who name His name. There can not be any further offering of the blood of bulls and goats, no more of a revival of the Old Testament priests offering sacrifices in a future Temple that will meet with God's approval. It would be an insult to Christ, who offered Himself *once and for all*, to be present if such is done. A future Temple will be for worship only, not sacrifices and offerings of blood by priests as a memorial. The memorial of the Lord's Supper will be over when Christ returns. No child of God would dare observe the ordinance of the "bread and cup" in Christ's presence. We do that "till He comes back," and any sacrifice that is repetitious of what was done in Old Testament days is of no significance.

Believers in Christ can thank God for the "Principle of the Priesthood" which enables us to go to God for our selves and hold up others before the throne of grace.

> *A Prayer Thought*
>
> Dear Lord, as I seek to practice my role as a priest today, may I permit the Holy Spirit to keep me holy and pure in thought, word and deed, kind one to another, honest in my dealings, forgiving one another, even as my High Priest has forgiven me. In His dear name, I pray. (Ephesians 4:32)

Chapter Four

THE PRINCIPLE OF LOVE

In the Second Chapter we saw in the *Principle of the Sacrifice* that God made a provision for any sinner to be saved by exercising faith in Christ. In the Third Chapter, the *Principle of the Priesthood*, He made those who have accepted Christ as their personal Savior His "chosen generation [race], a royal priesthood, a holy nation and a peculiar [special] people." Having been made *all* this in Christ, we are to "'show forth the praises of Him who has called us out of darkness into His marvelous light." (I Peter 2:9).

What better way to show forth our praise unto Him than by obeying His "Principle of Love." Moses told his hearers "You shall love the Lord your God with all your heart, with all your soul, and with all your mind" (Deuteronomy 6:5). Jesus reiterated this commandment and said," This is the first and great commandment." He added, "The second is like unto it, You shall love your neighbor as yourself. On these two laws hang all the laws of God" (Matthew 22:37–40). In this Chapter "Love" will be discussed in three parts: "God's" Love for Sinner and Saint;" "The Believer's Love for God;" and "The Believer's Love for His Neighbor."

Part I: God's Love for Us

In spite of man's sin and rebellion to truth, God's love has weathered every storm and weapon man has used against Him. Through the ages, His love has "suffered long." "In the time of Noah, His love suffered such depression under the weight of the world's iniquity that for a brief season it disappeared beneath the flood. Yet it still stood unbroken in the rushing torrent, and ever since has been reflected in the heavens in the 'bow of the rainbow covenant,' the pledge arid promise of the abiding character of that which it mirrors forth—His love."[7] The God of Christianity alone sets forth the Supreme Being of love. The gods of the heathen are angry, hateful beings and are in constant need of being appeased, often with abominable acts. Not so our God! *He is the Holy God of love.*

The Meaning of God's Love

It is that attribute or characteristic of God by which He seeks the highest good for all His creatures. In His love He seeks to have personal communion with each of them. His greatest act of love was demonstrated in the giving of His Son, the Lord Jesus Christ, to die for the sins of the whole world (John 3:16). Because God is perfect, His love is perfect. Because He is holy, His love is holy—holy and pure, and He seeks by His perfect and holy love to arouse man to his need of this love.

"To me this is the most profound of all truths—that the whole of the life of God is in the sacrifice of Himself, proving that God *is* love. Love involves sacrifice—to give rather than receive—the blessedness of self-giving. If the life of God were not such, it would be a falsehood to say that God is love. All the life of God is a flow of the divine self-giving love."[8]

God's Love for Sinners

God loves *all* sinners, the ungodly, those who are dead in sin. These people are not sinners because they sin, they sin because they are sinners. However, God loves His creatures in spite of their ungodliness and sin. It is their sin that He hates. The manifestation of His love is shown in making the infinite sacrifice of Christ for the salvation of those He loves. "For when we were helpless without strength, Christ died for the ungodly. One would hardly die for a righteous man, though perhaps for a good man someone would even dare to die. But God demonstrated His love for us in that while we were yet sinners, Christ died for us" (Romans 5:6–8). "When the wicked forsake their ways, and the unrighteous man his thoughts, let him return unto the Lord in penitence and in faith, and the God of love will have mercy upon him and will abundantly pardon" (Isaiah 55:7).

God will and does bestow full and complete pardon upon any penitent sinner who believes in His only begotten Son. He is not willing that any should perish but would have all men to be saved and come to a knowledge of the truth (II Peter 3:9b; I Timothy 2:3).

God's Love for Believers

Although God loves all mankind and sends the rain upon the just and unjust alike, He has a special and peculiar love for those who are united to Him by faith in His Son. His love makes provision for *all* our needs. It is hardly likely we could name them all, but here are a few:

1. When we are afflicted, He comes to our rescue (Psalm 34:17–19).
2. When we are distressed, His love manifests compassion (Psalm 86:15).
3. When He reveals His goodness to us, it shows His kindness (Psalm 117:2).
4. When tempted by that old serpent the devil, His love and faithfulness offers a way of escape (I Corinthians 10:13; James 1:2,3).

The Principle of Love

5. When Satan attacks, at our disposal is God's whole armor for victory (Ephesians 6:10–18).
6. When fiery trials come our way, His love provides a remedy that enables us to rejoice (I Peter 4:12,13; Romans 8:28).
7. His love has blessed us with *every* spiritual blessing in heavenly places in Christ Jesus. As we set our affection on things above where Christ is and not on things on the earth, our life is hid with Christ in God, and our *every need* will be supplied (Ephesians 1:4; Colossians 3:1,2; Philippians 4:19).

In the exercise of God's love for both sinner and saint, there are two necessities each needs—mercy and *grace*. Simply defined, mercy means "God's withholding what man deserves," and grace means "God's giving to man what he does not deserve." A sinner does not deserve God's salvation, but His love and mercy has made provision for it. Upon repentance and faith in Christ, God's grace gives this believer all he does not deserve—all that is necessary for him/her to have a personal relationship with Him and bestows assurance of eternal life in heaven with Him.

As Christ, who is now our Great High Priest, makes intercession for us, we are invoked, as we live for Him, to "come boldly before His throne of grace to obtain mercy and find grace to help in our time of need" (Hebrews 4:14–16). When king David sinned with Bathsheba, he confessed his sin to God (II Samuel 12:13). The Holy Spirit has been pleased to record the details of his confession for our benefit. In Psalm 51, David said, "Have mercy upon me according to Thy lovingkindness, according to the multitude of Thy tender mercies, blot out my transgressions" (sins—plural; vs. 1). His sins were multiple—adultery, putting the bottle to Uriah to make him drunk, and ordering Uriah's death to blame him for Bathsheba's pregnancy (II Samuel 11; Habakkuk 2:15). David knew what he deserved for his sins (Psalm 51:4). In his confession of guilt and deserving God's judgment, which carried with it death due to adultery, he asked for forgiveness according to God's love, compassion, and according to the *multitude* of God's tender mercies. He was asking God to withhold from him what he rightly deserved. Did God answer his prayer? David's 32nd Psalm says *yes*! God's grace gave him forgiveness which he did not deserve (vss. 1–5).

When we think of all that God has provided in and through His love and the mercy and grace which is available without our asking—accepting as a gift without price and without money, it is no wonder the Apostle Paul said man is without excuse" for his unbelief and not believing that salvation is by grace through faith and not by his works (Ephesians 2:8,9). With all these thoughts thus far in our consideration of God's love, especially for His children, we now consider-

Part II: Our Love for God

As we look back over the commandments Moses and Christ mentioned, they covered every facet of God's requirement for the members of His family. As a reminder we are to love Him with every fiber of our being, to walk in His ways and serve Him by keeping His statutes, which He commands of us *today* for our good (Deuteronomy 10:12,13).

These commandments leave no "loop holes" for us to deviate from them one iota. We are to love Him with every fiber of our being, to walk daily in every desire of God's heart for us. Our love is definitely contingent upon our obedience to His commandments and we are without excuse if we think we can manipulate any to suit our selfish desires.

One Greek New Testament word for love—agapao (agape) relates primarily to God's love—a divine love toward His Son and the human race, but it also has to do with the believer's love for God. The believer's love must have God for its primary object and express itself in complete obedience to His commandments. Another Greek word for love is *phileo* which represents *tender affection*. When Jesus asked Peter if he loved Him, He used the word *agape*. When Peter answered he used the word *phileo* (John 21:15).

In obeying God the different ways Moses and Christ described, God expects *agape*, not *phileo*. Love can only be known by the actions it prompts. To have less than *agape* is to put self first to be self-willed.

This is negative of a true love for God.

What then is implied in loving God *with all our heart, soul [life], mind* and *strength*, and when can it be said that a believer is doing all that God requires of him?

1. He loves God with all his *heart*, loving nothing in comparison of Him and nothing in reference to Him. He is ready to give up, do, suffer anything in order to please Him in every circumstance. This love permits God to regulate my life according to His schedule and His satisfaction. I saw an interesting saying in a Church bulletin that said: "Good morning, Robert, This is God speaking. I will be handling all your problems today. I will not need your help so, have a good day!" and then it closes with these two Bible verses: "Trust in the Lord with all your heart and lean not unto your own understanding. In all your ways acknowledge Him and He will direct your paths" (Proverbs 3:5,6). Submission to these verses will reveal that one is in obedience to God's commandments because of one's love for Him.

2. He loves God with all his soul—life. He is one who, if he saves himself—lives for self, will lose it. But if he loses it for the love for God, for Christ's sake, and the Gospel's, shall save it, proving he is a follower of Christ and an heir of eternal life (Mark 8:35). Regardless of what comes his way—trials, tribulation, etc., there is determination he will live for the Lord moment by moment. Jesus said the world hated Him and that it would hate his followers (John 15:18). Hate from the world, love from God!

Loving God with all one's heart is a principle that possibly originated with the saying, "The blood of the martyrs became the seed of the Church." These martyrs, beginning with the early New Testament saints and continues even 'till this day, show that the love these saints had for God was proof they loved not their own lives even unto death. No matter the hate the world had for them, they overcame the

The Principle of Love 37

world by the blood of the Lamb (Revelation 12:11). You and I may never be called upon to forfeit our lives for our faith in Christ and our love for our heavenly Father. We are called upon by Him to *live* for Him as a human sacrifice, wholly acceptable and a workman who needs not to be ashamed. This is a "Principle of Sacrifice." We obey it by not being worldly, by living in God's will (Romans 12:1,2).

3. He loves God with all his *strength*. Having become a co-laborer with God, he totally dedicates himself to give his all—the powers of his body in the service of his Master. Neither labor nor cost is spared. All his time, his goods, influence, talents, are on the altar of sacrifice to do a job well done for the One who gave His all for him.

4. He loves God with all his mind—his intellect—to know God, seeking His holy will as he follows in the footsteps of Jesus. This involves casting down imaginations and every high thing that exalts itself against the knowledge of God and bringing into captivity every thought to the obedience of Christ (II Corinthians 10:5). God has given unto us a "sound mind," even the very mind of Jesus Christ Himself, and we are to permit it to reveal His sacred truths (II Timothy 1:7; I Corinthians 2:16).

Our mind is tricky. There are times when it will wander and we must be so submissive to the Lord that we can banish from our natural understanding and memory every foolish, evil, dangerous thought and any idea which has a tendency to taint the heart and mind. Our mind must be set on things above where Christ is and not on things of this earth (Colossians 3:2). As we do this, we let the mind of Christ in us think on "things that are true, honest, just, pure, lovely, of a good report and anything worthy of praise to God." As we so think, the peace of God, which passes all understanding, will keep our hearts and minds through Christ—centered on spiritual matters (Philippians 4:7,8).

"He who sees God in all things, thinks of Him at all times, having his mind continually fixed on God, acknowledging Him in all his ways, who begins, continues and ends all his thoughts, words, and works to the glory of His name—this is the person who loves God with all his *heart, life, strength,* and *mind.* He is crucified to the world and the world to him. He lives, yet not he, but Christ in him."[9] This is the one person God is conforming to the image of His dear Son (Galatians 2:20).

A little boy knelt down by his mother's knees to say his prayers before going to bed. It was the usual "Now I lay me down to sleep" prayer and his asking God to bless mommy and daddy and the whole family, etc. After saying "Amen." he continued silently. His mother saw his lips moving and in a few moments he got up, She, wondering if he had done something wrong and was confessing it to the Lord, asked him what he had done. He simply said, "I was just telling God I loved Him." When was the last time you told Him you love Him?

Part III: "The Royal Principle."
Love Your Neighbor as Yourself

When Christ put His stamp of approval on the commandment Moses gave about the "Principle of Loving God," He hastened to add "The second is like unto it, thou shall love your neighbor as yourself (Matthew 22:39). James calls this law the "Royal Principle," possibly because it was given as such by the King of kings. Christ loved friend and enemy and He has set an example for us to love our fellow man. It truly is a "Royal Principle" not only because it was given by the King of kings because it was *commanded* by Him (James 2:8) The best way to love our neighbor as ourselves is to follow the *Golden Rule*, which is, "However you want people to treat you, so treat them" (Matthew 7:12). Rabbi Hillel of the first century said, "What is hateful to yourself, do not to someone else." Whether we like to admit it, we often take care of those we have a deep love for because we say "blood is thicker than water." There are those who have a deep love for and will go to any length to show we really care for them. These people we love as ourselves.

However, the Word of God teaches differently. Yes, there are some "neighbors" who live in sin, who ignore the claims of God upon them, and it is impossible to have fellowship with such. But Scripture presents a way we can show the love of Christ to them. We cannot love their sin, but we can love them because God loves them. In the Sermon on the Mount Jesus said, "Love your enemies, bless those who curse you, do good to those who hate you and pray for those who spitefully use you and persecute you that you may be recognized as a son of God your Father" (Matthew 5:44–46). We must have the right behavior before them so that they will be able to take knowledge that we have been with Jesus.

As we look further into the Word of God, we learn if a neighbor strikes us on the cheek turn the other cheek. If they compel us to go a mile with them, go two (Matthew 5:39–41). Paul says "Repay no evil for evil. Have regard for good things in the sight of all men. If possible, as far as it depends on you, live peaceably with all men. Do not take matters in your own hands and judge and punish an evil doer, but rather give place unto wrath. What does "rather give place to wrath" mean? *Never take it upon yourself to punish someone in your own hands. Stand back and let God punish*, for the Lord says, "Vengeance [judgment and punishment] is mine, I will repay." Paul then adds, "If your enemy is hungry, feed him. If he is thirsty, give him drink, for in so doing you will heap coals of fire upon his head" (Romans 12:17–20). What a wonderful way to show those who are our enemies that we truly have love for them.

What did Paul mean when he said if we make provisions for our enemy that would "heap coals of fire on his head?" This expression is also used in Proverbs 25:21,22. According to Adam Clarke, he says "the fire is not to consume, but to melt him into kindness; a metaphor taken from smelting metallic ores

> So artists melt the sullen ore of lead,
> By heaping coals of fire upon the head;
> In the kind warmth of metal learns to glow,
> And pure from dross, the silver runs before.

Another interpretation is that it refers to an ancient Egyptian custom in which a person who wanted to show public contrition carried a pan of burning coals upon his head. The coals represented the burning pain of his shame and guilt. When believers lovingly help their enemies, it should bring shame to such people for their hate and animosity.[10]

Our Responsibility to One Another[11]

—Be kindly affectioned one to another: Romans 12:10a; Ephesians 4:32a
—Prefer one another: Romans 12:10b
—Be of the same mind one toward another: Romans 12:16
—Edify one another: Romans 14:19; I Thessalonians 5:11
—Care one for another: I Corinthians 12:25.
—Bear one another's burdens: Galatians 6:2
—Lie not one to another: Colossians 2:9
—Speak not evil one to another: James 4:11
—Grudge not one against another: James 5:9
—Forebear one another: Ephesians 4:2
—Be tenderhearted one to another: Ephesians 4:32b
—Forgive one another: Ephesians 4:32c; Colossians 3:13
—Submit one to another: Ephesians 5:21
—Esteem other better than self: Philippians 2:3
—Teach, exhort one another: Colossians 3:16; Hebrews 3:13
—Comfort one another: I Thessalonians 4:18
—Consider one another: Hebrews 10:24
—Fellowship one with another: Hebrews 10:25a
—Confess faults one to another: James 5:16a
—Pray one for another: James 5:16b; I Samuel 12:23
—Have compassion one for another: I Peter 3:8
—Use hospitality one to another: I Peter 4:9
—Minister the same one to another: I Peter 4:10

The love that we have one for another, which fulfills the commandment of Christ, is a love of equity, charity, succor and benevolence. We owe to our neighbor what we have a right to expect from him. In a word, we must do everything in our power, through all the possible varieties of circumstances for our neighbors, which we would wish them to do for us if our situations were reversed. The list of twenty-three "one anothers" shows what the effect of our love will be for others when we put them into practice.

CONCLUSION

The Thirteenth Chapter of First Corinthians gives us a basic foundation for love. Three things stand out in regard to this subject. 1. God is *love*. 2. Christ and God are one, so Christ is *love*. 3. Every believer is in Christ, one with Him, so the believer is *love*. Without exercising our love we are but a noisy clanging cymbal, nothing, and even if we give all our goods to feed the poor and become a martyr, it profits nothing. But beginning with verse four through eight-a (NAS), we can substitute the word *God* for *love, Christ* for *love,* and *your name/my name* for *love.* Notice how you would read these verses as an "obedient test" if I used my name—Robert:

1. Robert is patient—not an agitator.
2. I am kind—not rude.
3. I am not jealous—not resentful.
4. I do not brag—not boastful.
5. I am not arrogant—not irritable.
6. I do not seek for self—not lustful or covetous.
7. I am not easily provoked—am meek with longsuffering.
8. I think no evil—not hypocritical.
9. I rejoice not in iniquity.
10. I rejoice in truth.
11. I bear up under all circumstances with Romans 8:28.
12. I believe all things spoken by God through His Word.
13. I hope all things, especially the "Blessed Hope" of Christ's return.
14. I endure all things since God is for me (Romans 8:31).

The next point is verse eight, "love never fails." As we look back over these points, having put our name in the place of love, what a challenge to love God and others as we ought. When we "live" this self will be completely out of the picture. We, then, will find ourselves revealing what is totally foreign to the world—a love that can come only from the heart of God and be relayed through ours.

A Prayer Thought

Dear God, when we think of Your love in our behalf, help us never to forget the length to which You went to redeem us from a devil's hell. Remind us daily that we are expected to show our love for You with all our heart, mind, soul and strength and in doing so, love our neighbor as ourselves. May we not love just in lip service but in truth and deed. In Jesus name. (I John 3:17,18)

Chapter Five

THE LORD'S PRINCIPLE: SANCTIFICATION AND LEAVEN

In Exodus, Chapters Twelve and Thirteen, several laws are given to Israel in regard to their keeping the Passover. Among these are (1) sanctifying the firstborn child and animal. The sanctifying of the firstborn child had to do with its being dedicated to God for whatever purpose He chose for the individual's service to Him. The sanctification of the firstborn animal was for the purpose of its sacrificial blood to atone for sin (2) The eating of unleaven bread. Leaven in this instance was a type of evil and was forbidden in any of its quarters.

Since *all* Scripture is given unto man and is profitable for doctrine . . . for instruction in righteousness (II Timothy 3:16), there are excellent spiritual applications in these two "Lord's Principles" for us to follow today (Exodus 13:9).

1. Sanctification (13:2). In a sense *sanctification* is a *law* for believers because we are informed, "This is the will of God, even your sanctification" (I Thessalonians 4:3). There is much controversy today in Christian circles over this subject of *sanctification*. We would like to discuss three views and then give the Bible definition.

    a. Holiness and Charismatic Groups state that after one is saved or justified by faith in Christ, there is a subsequent, second work of grace which eradicates the old carnal nature, baptizing one with the Holy Spirit. This usually enables the individual, now filled with the Holy Spirit to speak in tongues. With the carnal nature eradicated, if anything is done that is wrong, it is not a sin but a "mistake of the head and not of the heart." However, if one should sink back into sin, they could not only lose their sanctification but justification as well and then must be saved all over again.

    b. Conservative Groups generally believe sanctification means a gradual growth in grace and life on earth until perfection is attained—in heaven. It involves a steady, daily growth in grace and knowledge of Christ.

    c. Some Groups hold to the interpretation that sanctification means *suppression* of the old Adamic nature still within all believers, which suppression leads to a victorious life over the world, the flesh, and the devil.

d. The Bible definition is different from all three of the above, although the end result of Biblical sanctification includes total yieldedness, growth in grace and holiness and being filled with the Holy Spirit as brought out in Ephesians 5:18b. Sanctification simply means to be *set apart*—set apart unto God for His will to be performed in daily living. To get the proper meaning of the word *sanctify* or *sanctification*, apply all four definitions to; the following verses:[12]

—God sanctified the seventh day: Genesis 2:3
—Moses sanctified the firstborn infants: Exodus 13:2a
—Moses sanctified the first born animals: Exodus 13:2b
—Moses sanctified the people: Exodus 19:10
—Priests sanctified themselves: Exodus 19:22
—Moses sanctified Mount Sinai: Exodus 19:23
—God sanctified the Tabernacle: Exodus 29:43
—Moses sanctified the Tabernacle implements: Exodus 40:10,11
—Priests sanctified the house of God: II Chronicles 29:16,17
—God sanctified in "Gog" before heathens: Ezekiel 38:3,16
—A "fast" is sanctified: Joel 1:14
—Christ sanctified Himself: John 17:19
—Christ was sanctified by His Father: John 10:36
—Believers sanctify unbelievers: I Corinthians 7:14
—Believers are to sanctify God: I Peter 3:15

On the basis of the subjects just mentioned in relation to sanctification, the definitions listed in "a," "b" and "c" cannot possibly apply. The Holiness (a) interpretation relates only to a saved believer who has been sanctified, at which time their carnal nature is eradicated and they are then filled with the Holy Spirit. The Bible tells us that a *day, objects, things, animals, people by people, self, Christ, God*, and even *unbelievers* are sanctified. As stated, the simple definition of sanctification is to be *set apart*.

As we fulfill the Word of God in our lives by "setting ourselves apart" unto Him, we see that "God has not called us unto uncleanness, *but unto holiness*" (II Thessalonians 4:3,7). According to the foreknowledge of God, we were chosen in Him before the foundation of the world to be holy and without blame before Him in love (Ephesians 1:4). We exhibit a holy life by,[13]

1. Being dead to sin but alive unto God: Romans 6:11
2. Yieldedness to His will: Romans 6:13
3. Complete dedication: Romans 12:1,2
4. Surrender: Luke 9:23
5. Separation: II Corinthians 6:16,17
6. Abiding in Christ: John 15:7; Philippians 1:21a
7. Obedience to Christ's commands: Matthew 9:9; John 15:14

We are sanctified (set apart unto godly, holy living)[14]

The Lord's Principle: Sanctification and Leaven 43

    1. By God the Father: Jude 1
    2. By the offering of Christ: Hebrews 10:10
    3. By the blood of Christ: Hebrews 13:12,13
    4. By the Holy Spirit: I Corinthians 6:11
    5. By faith: Acts 26:18
    6. Through truth: John 17:17
    7. Being sanctified, we are perfected *forever*: Hebrews 10:14

"The sanctification of the Spirit commences in regeneration, it is carried through life and it will be complete in the day of Christ. It consists in making us holy, or inwardly and outwardly conforming us to the likeness of the Lord Jesus Christ. It separates us from the world, sets our hearts against sin, consecrates us to the Lord's service, makes us zealous for His glory, and creates us anew in Christ. Physically, we are the same as before but morally and spiritually we differ greatly. The more we experience the sanctifying work of the Spirit, the more clearly we shall discover our own sinfulness, the more we shall be tried with our inward corruptions, the more we shall see the need of the Savior's blood, the more we shall bless God for the Redeemer's finished work on Calvary, and the more carefully and cautiously we shall walk in our pilgrimage journey in this ungodly, evil world. Nothing will prove our calling by the Father or our redemption by the Son but being sanctified—set apart by the Holy Spirit."

2. Leaven as Evil. Having considered the "Lord's Principle" in relation to sanctification, Moses mentioned a second law to be considered, that of not eating any *leavened bread—only unleavened* bread during the seven day feast of the Passover (13:3,6,9). Leaven in these feasts represented evil and corruption. In the case of the Passover, the unleaven bread was a type of Christ as our Passover, our sinless Savior who had no sin, evil or corruption (I Corinthians 5:7; Hebrews 4:15). Unleavened bread is a symbol of sincerity and truth (I Corinthians 5:8a).

As we approach the New Testament, in each instance but one, leaven is a symbol of evil—especially the legalism and hypocrisy of Phariseeism and immoral practices throughout the world (I Corinthians 5:8b). Believers need to be constantly aware of the evilness of *leaven* and make sure that each step be ordered in God's Word so that no iniquity will be found in them (Psalm 119:133).

We are told to "Love not the world, neither the things that are in the world. If any man love the world the love of the Father is not in him. For all that is in the world, the lust of the flesh, the lust of the eyes and the pride of life is not of the Father but of the world. And the world passes away and the lusts also, but he who does God's will abides forever" (I John 2:15–17). These verses are telling us that *anything* of the world, the flesh and the devil is like leaven which will work through us if the Scriptures do not have preeminence in our lives. The Apostle Paul gave a good proverb: "A little yeast works through the whole batch of dough" (Galatians 5:9 NIV). The warning of leaven has to do with sin in the life of the believer plus the contradictory teachings of false prophets in our midst (Matthew 7:15; 24:11; Mark 13:22; I Peter 4:1).

In spite of our position in Christ, we are still in the flesh. Although we possess God's divine nature and are His heirs and joint heirs with Jesus Christ (II Peter 1:4; Romans 8:17), there are times when I desire to do good but the evil I shouldn't do, I do. I delight in the law of God after the inward man but there is a law working against the law of my mind and brings me into captivity to the law of sin. Our only deliverance from this *leaven* of sin, this evil, is none other than Christ who enables us to serve God's Principle of Unleaven (Romans 7:15–25).

There are so many promises in the Word of God that can come to our rescue when leaven seeks to permeate our being. Christ warns us to beware of the leaven of the Pharisees lest we substitute tradition for the Word of God. One excellent promise to cling to when evil rears its ugly head is: "There has no temptation taken you but what is common to man." Never entertain the thought that you alone are going through something no one else has. But continuing the verse, Paul says, "God is faithful who will not allow or permit you to be tempted beyond what you are able [or to the breaking point], but will with that temptation make a way of escape so that you will be able to bear it" (I Corinthians 10:13). Proverbs warns us "Not to go in the path of the wicked and go not in the way of evil men" (4:14). We are told to avoid those who cause divisions and offenses contrary to the doctrine which we have learned (Romans 16:17).

Whatever comes our way that causes us to take our eyes off Jesus and indulge in the "leaven" of wickedness will make us a stumbling block to others. We cannot give God 99 rooms of our heart and keep one for self. That is not total dedication. By so doing, our one room will soon become too small and we will want to expand. Leaven's desire is to take the whole and unless we face the fact of really backsliding, we must not try to cover our evil but *confess* and *forsake* it and give God all the rooms of our heart and life. Only then will we receive His mercy and forgiveness (Proverbs 28:13).

Satan has been in business for over 6,000 years and nothing delights him more than to lead a believer into temptation and then "push" him into the yielding to that temptation. His wiles of deceit are second to none. He can appear as an angel of light, causing false prophets to transform themselves into apostles of Christ and as ministers of righteousness (II Corinthians 11:13–15). These deceitful workers can so twist Scripture that before one knows it, we become something like Eve and "take a bite." The leaven can spread so quickly that before we know it we begin to have a "pity party" and are ready to throw in the sponge. But if we are willing to practice our sanctification and set our whole being apart unto the Lord, we will be so fortified with the Word of God that we can follow the prophet Jeremiah's example when he was so under the fire of opposition of his own backslidden people. He wanted to quit but said "The Word of God was in my heart as a burning fire shut up in my bones. I was weary but I couldn't quit." He had previously said, "Your words were found and I did eat them" (20:9; 15:16). Old suffering Job said, "Neither have I gone back from the commandment of His lips. I have esteemed the words of His mouth more than my necessary food" (23:12). God help us to have this kind of testimony. We can if we consider spiritual food more necesary than physical.

The Lord's Principle: Sanctification and Leaven 45

In the establishment of the Passover and the requirement of Israel setting herself apart unto God and not contaminating the feast of the Passover with leaven bread, we can see God's desire for the Israelites to set a proper example before their children and their children's children. Not only that, but He wanted Israel to let others know that they were a people called by His name (Deuteronomy 28:9,10). Righteousness exalts a nation but sin is a reproach to any people (Proverbs 14:34).

3. Leaven as Good. In making a study of *leaven* I have been surprised at the number of fundamental scholars who say that throughout the Bible leaven always represents evil, possibly because it produces fermentation. Yes, leaven does permeate all that it contacts, but it does not stand for evil in every instance. The fact that Israel could eat only unleavened bread during the week of the feast of the Passover definitely implies that God permitted them to eat leavened bread prior to and after this feast. Leaven works itself through the whole until everything is affected, whether for good or for evil. We have seen in some instances how it works for evil, so let us take notice how it can and does work for good.

a. Leaven was used in bread as an offering with the sacrifice of thanksgiving of the peace offering (Leviticus 7:13). This *good* leaven could be applied to Paul's "law" of thanksgiving. "In everything give thanks for this is the will of God in Christ Jesus concerning you" (I Thessalonians 5:17).

The prophet Amos tells us that leaven was required as part of a thanksgiving offering or sacrifice (4:6). The more leaven we use in this sacrifice of thanksgiving, it shows how thankful we are to the Lord for His goodness to us. "O that men would praise the Lord for His goodness" (Psalm 107:8 with 23:6).

b. In what is called the "Feast of the Weeks," a harvest feast known as Pentecost was observed. Two loaves, baked with fine flour and *leaven* were brought as first fruits unto the Lord (Leviticus 23:17,18). The first fruits are symbolic of a harvest of seeds that were sown in the ground and died, but upon dying, they brought forth much fruit (John 12:24). This wave loaf baked with leaven speaks to us of Christ being our first fruits—His resurrection from the dead (I Corinthians 15:20).

c. Christ said "The kingdom of heaven is like unto leaven" (Matthew 13:33). Can you imagine Christ saying this if leaven were evil? In this one verse alone Jesus contradicts the scholars who say that leaven throughout the Scriptures stands for evil. As leaven expands the dough, in the case of Jesus' remark, leaven symbolizes the permeating effect of the Gospel of Jesus Christ throughout the world. The Book of Acts gives an excellent example of the preaching of the kingdom of heaven/God sweeping across Asia Minor and into several countries of Europe. In spite of the perilous times in which we live, those who are faithful in preaching the Gospel and believers who still stand for the truth still see results of the *leaven* of the Gospel taking effect in the lives of those who believe on the Lord Jesus Christ and are saved. Believers are definitely outnumbered when compared to the population of the world but God has always had a remnant who like Paul "press toward the mark for the prize of the high calling of God in Christ Jesus" (Philippians 3:14).

We can learn a good lesson when Christ told Peter he would deny Him three times (Luke 22:31–34). Peter was told that Satan desired to have him that he might sift him as wheat (vs. 32). When wheat was sifted the chaff was blown into the air and was separated from the wheat (or fruit). Satan wanted to exhibit Peter's chaff or imperfections so that onlookers would see that a follower of Christ had the potential to bring shame to his Lord and Savior. With Satan's attack imminent, Jesus told Peter, "But I have prayed for you" (vs. 32).

One lesson to be learned in this incident is that prayer is reciprocal. We send *up* our prayers to God and ask for an answer, which often He sends down from heaven. With Christ ever living to make intercession for us, He is also praying for us that our faith fail not. We need to put our name in the place of Peter's and realize that Jesus is speaking to us and that He expects us to answer His prayer that *our* faith fail not. He sends *down* His prayer to us and He expects us to send our answer *up* to Him. I often wondered if God didn't answer our prayers like we answer His, where would we be today? Old Peter was contaminated with a "loaf of *evil* leaven bread" and failed to answer Christ's prayer in denying Him three times. However, in due process of time, Peter wept for his sin and was a definite answer to Christ's prayer on the Day of Pentecost.

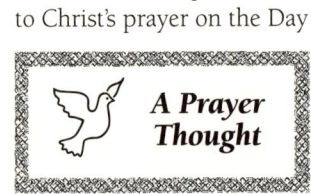

A Prayer Thought

One last thought. Jesus said "When I come, will I find faith?" (Luke 18:8). That depends, of course, if we are a living answer to His prayer. If we permit the "good leaven" to "work its way through the whole batch of dough," He will (Galatians 5:9).

Dear Heavenly Father, I am so thankful You are keeping me in Your hand. When Satan attacks me because I belong to You, help me to do what Your Son did when He was tempted by saying, "Get thee behind Me Satan." Help me to apply the good leaven of the Gospel by using Your strength day by day to keep the faith. In Christ's name I pray, Amen. (Romans 14:23b; James 2:20)

Chapter Six

THE PRINCIPLE OF FORGIVENESS

It has been said the two most important words in any language are "I'm sorry." As important as these two words are, there are two other most important words: "I forgive." What a different world we would be living in if everyone had a forgiving spirit. This study will be divided into two parts:

1. To show that God is love, that He will forgive any sinner who comes to Him in penitence and faith to receive the Lord Jesus Christ as his own personal Savior and that He will forgive any child of His when there is true repentance, confession, and forsaking of sin.

2. To show the result of unforgiven sin on the believer's part toward a brother or sister in Christ, and how to get victory over sin and be restored, not only to fellowship with God but fellowship with the accused. To forgive is to set a prisoner free and discover that the prisoner is *you*.

God's Forgiveness of a Sinner

Forgiveness applies to sin—a sin committed against self, others, and of course, God. When Joseph was enticed by Potiphar's wife to commit adultery, he replied, "How then can I do this great wickedness *and sin against God?*" (Genesis 39:9). When David had his affair with Bathsheba and had her husband murdered, he said in his confession, "Against You [God] and You only have I sinned" (Psalm 51:4). All sin is against God, but it also involves others—some guilty—some innocent.

No matter what the sin is, God sees it as sin. In His eyes there is no such thing as small, medium, large, or giant size sins. We are the ones who categorize sin, not God. A lie is a sin, whether it is white or black, whether it is big or small. A good moral but unsaved baptized Church member will share the same hell with a rank ungodly criminal (Revelation 21:8). All have sinned and come short of the glory of God and if there is never any acceptance of Christ, no matter how good their works might be, they will be denied by Christ saying unto them, "I never knew you!" (Matthew 7:21–25). All have been shaped in iniquity and conceived in sin, We sin because we are sinners not sinners because we sin. This leaves us without any standing before a holy and righteous God. To be forgiven that we might be accepted by God, His "Principle of Forgiveness" must be applied to each individual heart. As sinners we owe a debt we cannot pay, but God, who is rich in mercy. allowed His son to pay our debt, which He didn't owe. And because He died for the sins of the world—including *mine*, I must confess that I am a sinner and trust Christ for forgiveness, which He made possible through the shedding of His own precious blood. If we say we have not sinned, we lie, we deceive ourselves. But if we confess our sins He is faithful and just to forgive us our sins and to cleanse us from all unrighteousness" (I John 1:9). I know this verse refers primarily to a Christian, but it applies equally as well to a sinner who comes to Christ.

God's desire is to save souls and forgive sin, and when any sinner comes to Him through Christ, "he shall not come into judgment but is passed from death unto life." "He that believeth on Him is not condemned" (John 3:18; 5:24; Acts 16:31; Romans 10:9,10).

God's Forgiveness for Christians

Nowhere does the Bible teach "Sinless Perfection" for a believer. "Saints" in the Church at Corinth were anything but saints in outward testimony. Some of the believers in the Church at Ephesus were lying, stealing and using corrupt language (Ephesians 4:25–29). For us to say we have not sinned since we were saved is to lie, and if we make such a statement, we just told a lie! (I John 1:6,8).

Since we do sin, are we to categorize them? Are we to overlook some and confess others? Shall we try to hide them as though that were possible? We have stated that a "little white lie" is as big as a "big black lie." An evil thought is a sin. Harboring an unforgiving spirit or having enmity against a brother, is a sin. Stealing, adultery, anger, jealously, envy, etc., are sins. But no matter the sins, true confession makes it right and God does and will forgive. As I look at my own life, I wonder why God ever forgave me, but He did and thankfully when I did confess my sins to Him His forgiveness was for Christ's sake (I John 1:9; Ephesians 4:32).

Someone might ask" "Is there forgiveness for something called big or anything that has really done damage to others that causes grief?" If God has ever forgiven you of *any* sin, it was big—it hurt and grieved Him. But you confessed and expected forgiveness. He did it on the basis of your confession. He said He would and you took Him at His word, believing you were forgiven. If we cover our sins we can confess all day and forgiveness isn't granted. Why? "He who covers his sins shall not prosper [is defeated] but whosoever confesses *and forsakes* them shall have mercy [forgiveness] (Proverbs 28:13).

In the strictest sense of the word we do not have to ask for forgiveness. Forgiveness is automatically granted when we rightly confess. It is a matter of accepting it by faith. First John 1:9 doesn't say "He is faithful and just to forgive us *if we ask Him to*," but He will forgive and cleanse us the moment we confess. Forgiveness is settled. It has been granted. We do not have to ask for something that is already ours. His forgiveness was on the basis of the blood Christ shed at Calvary, which cleansed us for our sin and our forgiveness is for Christ's sake.

There are three things a believer ought always to remember in the matter of sin, repentance and confession:

The Principle of Forgiveness 49

1. Confession means to declare openly before God the fact of your sin, spelling it out, and upon His forgiveness, confess freely to anyone involved in the act of your sin. If you lied *spell it out* to God, He does not forgive on the basis of *if I have sinned*. David's confession was correct. He confessed to his awful wrong of transgression—his acts of sin with Bathsheba and ordering her husband killed. He confessed to his iniquity, the fact that he was a sinner and had sinned. He confessed the fact that he had put down the authority of God's Word and had belittled God Himself (II Samuel 12:9,10; Psalm 53:1–3). God forgave him, based upon the type of confession made in Psalm 32:1–5. Keep in mind that the Psalms are not written in chronological order. Moses' Psalm is 90 and David's confession in Psalm 51 is before his testimony in Psalm 32:1–5. With confession and forgiveness comes restoration of fellowship with and service for God, as David experienced. (See II Samuel 12:26–31 with I John 1:7 based upon I John 1:9).

2. What does God do with our sins when they are confessed according to His "Principle of Forgiveness"? He-[15]

—Lays them upon Christ: Isaiah 53:6; I Peter 2:24
—Washes them away: Revelation 1:5
—Forgives and covers them: Romans 4:7
—Casts them behind His back: Isaiah 38:17b
—Casts them in the depth of the sea: Micah 7:19b
—Removes them as far as the east is from the west: Psalm 103:12
—Blots them out: Isaiah 43:25a
—Remembers them no more: Isaiah 43:25b; Hebrews 8:12

3. We sing a song titled "Calvary Covers it All." It does when it comes to forgiveness of sin and having them blotted out. But Calvary does not make atonement for the consequences of sin. "Whatsoever a man sows, that shall he also reap" (Galatians 6:7). The "sword" of reaping *never* left David's house during his lifetime (II Samuel 12:10–12). David truly repented and was forgiven, but his acts were costly. We not only reap what we sow, we reap more than we sow. David lost *four* of his sons as a result of having *one* Uriah killed. So many of us learn this lesson the hard way. God does give mercy and grace to help and sustain us in our reaping, and for this we can praise Him over and over. Our reaping the consequences of our sin should be a deterrent in the matter of our disobedience. One does not put his finger on a hot stove *twice* to see if it's still hot!

Our Forgiveness of Others

One of the greatest tests of our salvation is whether we love the brethren. In John's First Epistle he said this: "We know we have passed from death if we love the brethren. He who loves not his brother abides in death. Whosoever hates his brother is a murderer and we know that no murderer has eternal life abiding in him (3:15,16). One of the implications here is that a Christian loves his brother—he always has a forgiving spirit toward him.

Forgiveness toward others is not the easiest thing to do. Ever hear someone say, After all he's done to me, forgive him? "Are you serious?" I'll never forgive him" or "If I do forgive him, I'll never forget what he did to me." Such remarks come from a babe in Christ, one who hasn't grown up yet. He does not fully understand what the Scripture teaches about forgiving one another.

Forgiving a fellow believer is setting someone free from the responsibility that is theirs because of the wrong done against us. A debt is forgiven when it is paid in full. People who suffer from an unforgiving spirit do not fully realize that their problem is unforgiveness.

Results of an Unforgiving Spirit

An unforgiving spirit breaks communication with the so-called guilty party. If anything is said, it is usually with malice, and tempers are "found," not lost. Bitterness reigns, God's Spirit is grieved, Christlikeness is foregone, and the person who should be loved is despised. Such feelings and behavior patterns indicate these people have not come to grips with the full teaching of God's forgiveness and all the implications of forgiveness. The one truth that has no authority in their lives is "Be ye kind one toward another, forgiving one another, even as God for Christ's sake has forgiven you" (Ephesians 4:32).

An unforgiving person is always the loser in life, much more so than the one he holds a grudge against. His attitude proves he's walking after the flesh instead of the Spirit. In due process of time one relationship creates other relationships, which are not harmonious to Christian behavior. A wrong attitude of forgiveness sometimes leads to bitterness and false accusations increase. What they don't realize is that they become hostage to themselves. A game of waiting is played, expecting the other party to come and make an apology. No effort is made up their part to make amends.

All bitterness, wrath, anger, and evil speaking against the one you have wronged must be put away, malice included (Ephesians 4:31). Only then can one be kind and forgiving (Ephesians 4:32) Unforgiveness is sin. It is disobedience and must be confessed and forgiven. Why expect the Lord to forgive us of any sin when bitterness keeps us from forgiving the one we say has wronged us? If we don't put away bitterness it can affect us physically. It affected Naomi's facial features (Ruth 1:19,20). It can even affect one's bones (Psalm 17:22b; 32:3). It can also affect us spiritually. It affects our love for God (I John 4:20,21). The bitterness of sin can hinder our spiritual progress (Hebrews 12:1). It creates an empty life, permitting depression to set in. Depression makes one feel so low they have to look up to see bottom. Another consequence of unforgiveness is that one's bitterness is passed on from one generation to another (Exodus 34:7).

Getting Victory over Unforgiveness

1. Repent of carnal practices and a lack of love. We are to love our enemies, give our cloak to those who ask, and walk the second mile with our brother if necessary. It is better to do the "extra" and be rid of bitterness and a guilty conscience than harbor unforgiveness and not lend a helping hand.

The Principle of Forgiveness 51

2. View the offender as one of God's instruments. He, too, is a co-laborer with God, your blood-bought brother in Christ. There must be recognition that we must learn to live together with people down here on earth who we will have to live with in heaven. And who knows, you just might have to live next door to the fellow you wouldn't forgive!

3. Thank God for His purpose through each offense, knowing that He is permitting all things to work together for our best interest, and that in each situation His grace is available and sufficient for us.

4. Search our hearts for any wrong attitudes and seek motivations for right attitudes. "Accentuate the positive and eliminate the negative."

5. Focus on what God has done *for* us and not what we think the other fellow has done *to* us. If we don't we could pace the floor each night while the "unforgiving person" is sleeping like a log!

6. Consider what we think the other fellow is entitled to from us, and then remember that God will withhold no good thing from those who walk uprightly.

So much more could be said about an unforgiving spirit but suffice it to say, the person with this type of spirit must come to grips with his attitudes as difficult as they may seem to be, as hard as they need to be changed. He must see that sin is like a cancer that can spread throughout his whole system. He must face up to the truth that in Christ he is dead to self, that he has been crucified with Christ. This means that "Being dead to self, (1) no one can hurt a dead person; (2) no dead person has any feelings; (3) no dead person has any reputation, so there is nothing to fight about; (4) no dead person has any selfish ambition, so he has nothing to be bitter, angry, jealous or unforgiving about; (5) no dead person has any possessions, so he has nothing to lose or worry about; (6) no dead person has any rights, so he can suffer no wrong, and (7) he is already dead so no one can kill him."[16]

Whatever wrong that created an unforgiving spirit there is no sin so big that God will not forgive. Again may we remind ourselves that God's Word teaches us that we are to "Forgive one another, even as God for Christ's sake has forgiven us" (Ephesians 4:32).

CONCLUSION

Forgiveness will heal any situation. Unforgiveness festers the situation, causing busy-bodies to openly criticize, heaping condemnation on the wrong person. And what does God think of unforgiveness? He forgives us as we forgive one another (Matthew 6:14,15; Mark 11:25; Luke 6:37). On the basis of these verses, He does not condone unforgiveness.

Punishment for unforgiveness will be greater than one realizes. In the "Principle of Forgiveness" (Matthew 18:21–3) Jesus concludes His discourse by saying that if one does not forgive, he/she will be delivered unto the "tormentors" until things are made right. "Tormentor" refers to one's conscience that seeks to justify one's unforgiving spirit. One's "tormentor" finds no rest till things are made right with God. By confessing wrong and proving they were sorry for being unforgiving is a spiritual accomplishment of the highest magnitude, thus showing spiritual maturity. We must point out that the innocent party must also have a forgiving spirit.

The Pharisees were eager to condemn a woman taken in adultery. This sin, even in the eyes of God, cannot be taken lightly. It is condemned so often in the Scriptures. However, Jesus, in John 8:1–11, made two important points in relation to this incident.

1. When the Pharisees brought this woman to Jesus, He revealed to them that judging someone when they themselves had sin in their lives, was wrong. This is why He said to them, "He that is without sin let him cast the first stone." Being guilty, they made a hasty exit.

2. He revealed that the "Principle of Forgiveness" made it possible for her sins to be forgiven by saying, "Neither do I condemn you, go, sin no more."

If there is a willingness to forgive, this is the first step that needs to be taken. If there is no willingness, the unforgiving party is just as guilty before God, if not more so, than the one being accused. Two sins do not make a right. The decision rests with the one who says they have been wronged and have an attitude of unforgiveness.

There is another side of the "Coin of Forgiveness." Jesus said, "Take heed to yourself; if your brother (or anyone) trespass against you, rebuke him [show him his wrong] and if he repents, forgive him" (Luke 17:3). To do otherwise is to sin grossly, at least as much as the guilty one. This makes both parties guilty before the Lord and puts the first guilty person in a position where he must be willing to forgive the second guilty party. It looks like the Lord has us coming and going in the matter of forgiveness. We must all forgive whether we are wrong or whether we are the ones wronged, and do it for Christ's sake.

True forgiveness comes when we get right first, first with God and then in all humility make things right with the other person, *never* to bring up the subject again. It is saying, "I have been convicted of my sin of unforgiveness by God's Spirit. I was wrong in my thoughts and attitudes about you, the mean things I said about you, and I'm asking you to please forgive me." The words expressed must be the right ones. The timing must be right also, not during the time of hardness of heart, rebellion and refusal to make amends. Anything said then would be hypocritical. But being gripped and led by the Holy Spirit, that is the time to go to our brother, make confession, making things right and asking for forgiveness.

There are times, being human, that we ourselves might remember the wrong, but in forgiveness all bitterness and hurt are under the blood. When you said, "I'm sorry," you had to mean it and drop the subject. It can be done since "we can do all things through Christ who strengthens us" (Philippians 4:13). As someone put it, "We forgive and forget, then forget what we forgave."

As we look at the challenge Christ gave to Peter when he asked how often he should forgive, he was told, "seventy times seven" (Matthew 18:21,22). Peter no doubt thought forgiving seven times was noble and generous, but the answer he got must have staggered his imagination. Why forgive 489 times more if

A Prayer Thought

The Principle of Forgiveness

one did it once and really meant it? I believe the underlying meaning here is that the spirit of forgiveness should be perpetual, unending. Paul gives us a good word of advice to close the matter: "Forbearing one another and forgiving one another. If any man have a quarrel against any, even so as Christ forgave you, you do likewise" (Colossians 3:13).

> Dear Lord, when we think that in You we have forgiveness through the blood of Your dear Son, help us moment by moment to remember that the forgiveness You have bestowed upon us to become right with You must be exhibited toward others, that we must be right with them and they must be right with us. Help us to keep the past buried and the present alive with love one for another. In Jesus name, Amen. (Ephesians 4:32 with Hebrews 10:24)

Chapter Seven

THE PRINCIPLE OF PRAYER

The term "prayer" as used in its largest sense includes all forms of communication with God. It embraces worship, praise, thanksgiving, supplication and intercession. The definite teaching as found in the Scriptures on the subject of prayer deals principally with the last two aspects—supplication and intercession.

With prayer being our means of communication with God for the above purposes mentioned, it is no wonder we find such commands or laws as "Men ought always to pray and faint not." We should "pray without ceasing" (Luke 18:1; I Thessalonians 5:17). We are not to be anxious about anything, but in *everything* by prayer and supplication *with* thanksgiving we are to make our request made known unto God (Philippians 4:6).

What is Real Prayer[17]
- —It is that God might be glorified in the answer.
- —One does not pray to change God's mind or will, but for God to adjust us to His will.
- —It is permissible for one to pray for whatever is permissible to desire.
- —Prayer is not so much the getting of answers as it is getting a hold of the God who answers prayer.
- —Our ability to stay with God in the prayer closet is the measure of our ability to stay with God when we are outside the prayer closet.
- —An attitude of prayer will create an atmosphere of prayer.
- —Prayer is the atmosphere in which all Christian virtues grow.
- —Prayer is a golden river at whose brink some die of thirst, while others kneel and drink.
- —Kneeing in prayer will always keep one in good standing with God.
- —A saint can see farther on his knees than a philosopher can on his tiptoes.
- —The devil is no match for a saint on his knees who is depending upon God for His strength and power.
- —Seven days without prayer makes one *weak*.
- —If you are too busy to pray, you are too busy.

—Prayer is weakness leaning on Omnipotence.
—Prayer is faith laying hold on God's promises.
—Prayer is the thirsty soul crying for Living Water.
—Prayer is a virtue that prevails against temptation.
—Prayer is the Christian's staff by which he is helped along life's pathway.
—Prayer is the believer's outstretched hand and upward vision seeking the fulness of God.
—Prayer is the child taking God's hand for His leading.
—Prayer is inspiration accepting the challenge to lay hold of Divine realities.
—Prayer is the open door by which the individual may pass from struggle to victory.
—Prayer is God's instrument by which one's tribulations become patience.
—Prayer, coupled with faith, is trusting God in the dark.
—The end of worry is prayer. The end of prayer is peace.
—Prayer is not a *snap* course for snap answers. We cannot *rush* God in our praying. We do not ask God for patience and then say, "Hurry up with the answer."
—God answers prayer in three ways: *Yes, No,* and *Wait.*
—Much *prayer—much power,* little *prayer—little power,* no prayer—no power.
—The importance of prayer can be measured only by the prominence of it in the Scriptures and in the lives of those who have been used by God.

We need only to look into the lives of several Bible characters to see the importance of prayer.

1. Prayer of Hannah, Samuel's mother. Her problems were typical of many homes today (I Samuel 1:1;2:10).[18]

—There were divisions between members: 1:1–7.
—She was misunderstood by her husband: 1:8.
—She was bitter: 1:10.
—But she prayed for help and made a vow to the Lord: 1:9–11.
—She was misunderstood by her pastor: 1:12–16.
—Her prayer was answered: 1:19–23.
—She then presented her all to the Lord: 1:24–28; Mark 12:41–44.

Result of Her Answered Prayer
—She praised God for His goodness to her as a mother: 2:1–9.
—She named her son "Samuel" which meant *asked of God*: 1:20.
—Samuel followed her example of praying and his prayer brought victory for Israel at Mizpah against the Philistines: 7:5–11.
—He continually prayed for Israel: 12:23.

The Principle of Prayer

Lesson: "Trust in the Lord with all your heart and lean not to your own understanding. In all your ways acknowledge Him and He will direct and make straight your path" (Proverbs 3:5,6).

2. Nehemiah, a "prayer warrior" with determination. Jerusalem had been destroyed by Nebuchadnezzar and after Israel's seventy year Babylonian Captivity, when Nehemiah learned of the devastated ruins of his beloved city, he immediately went to the Lord in prayer (Nehemiah 1:4–11). So burdened was he for Jerusalem to be rebuilt he prayed to God that king Artaxerxes would give him permission to return to Jerusalem and complete the job. God used the king to grant Nehemiah's request.

The How of Nehemiah's Prayer[19]
- —It was *earnest*—accompanied by fasting which continued both day and night: 1:4.
- —It was *hopeful*, looking to God's faithfulness and mercy: 1:5, 6a.
- —It was *humble*, accompanied by confession of sin: 1:1,6b,8.
- —It was *believing*, claiming God's promise to the repentant and obedient:1:9.
- —It was *practical* and *unselfish*, a particular object in view for his nation and countrymen, benefitting himself only remotely: 1:10,11.
- —It was *stimulating*, inspiring Nehemiah to take steps toward answering his own prayer to rebuild the city walls: 2:4b, 5.
- —It was *successful*, the king granted him permission to leave: 2:2:8b.
- —It was *God glorifying*, "according to the good hand of my God upon me:" 2:8b.

Nehemiah's ringing testimony led the Israelites to "have a mind to work" with him in reconstruction of the city wall. Though they met with much opposition, Nehemiah prayed again and a watch was set to take care of their enemies (4:8,9).

Lesson: In answer to prayer, the wall was completely rebuilt (Ch. 3; 6:15). When we pray for God's will to be accomplished according to the pattern of Nehemiah, we can be assured that if we ask anything according to His will, He not only *hears* us but *grants* the petition we desire of Him (I John 5:14,15).

3. The Apostle Paul. In Paul's Epistles he made mention at least eighteen times that believers are *members one of another* (Ephesians 4:25b). One in particular is that as a child of God we are to *pray one for another* (Ephesians 4:25b). He gives us his testimony of his praying in behalf of others.[20]

- —For the Romans, he prays for *edification*: 1:9–12.
- —For the Ephesians, he prays for *enlightment* and *power*: 1:15–19.
- —For the Philippians, he prays for *fellowship*: 1:3–5.
- —For the Colossians, he prays for a *worthy walk*: 1:9–11.

—For the Thessalonians he prays for *service*, their *work* of faith and their *labor* of live (I) 1:23, and for *growth in grace* (II) 1:3,4.
—For Timothy, he prays for him to *stir up his gift* (II) 1:3–6.
—For Philemon, he prays he might *communicate his faith*: vss. 4–6.

Lesson: Every believer needs the prayers of his brother and sister in Christ. It could be for a personal or family problem, sickness, death, etc. To ignore the needs of others and not uphold them before the throne of grace is definitely a matter of breaking the "Principle of Prayer and Love." A good example of this is remembering a fellow believer. When Herod threatened Peter with imprisonment and death for his faith, immediately the Church members prayed for him without ceasing, which resulted in his release from prison (Acts 12:1–16). *Prayer changes things.* It not only changes things but it changes people and they change things.

The three examples of the Old and New Testament saints have set a good pattern for us in the things for which we should pray. It seems that in our day and age we talk *much* about prayer but we don't take the time we should to pray. "Family Altars" are a thing of the past, and as a result of our not having a home time for devotions, many Christians are content that there are closed doors to a Wednesday Night Prayer Meeting in many Churches. It is no wonder that there is such little Christian influence in our land today. Daniel, Peter and John were faithful in their prayer time—Daniel praying three times daily and Peter and John went to the Temple "at the ninth hour" to pray (Daniel 6:10; Acts 3:1). Even Christ took time to pray (Mark 6:46).

"What the Church needs today is not more machinery or better, not new organizations, or more and novel methods, but men whom the Holy Spirit can use, men of prayer, mighty men of prayer. The Holy Spirit does not flow through methods but *individuals*. He does not come upon machinery but on *people*. He does not anoint plans but people—*people of prayer*. Talking to others for God is one thing, but talking to God *for* people is greater still. One will never talk well and with real success to others *for* God who has not learned well how to talk *to* God for them."[21] This lesson the early Church knew. They did not ask the Lord to teach them *how* to pray, but "Lord teach us *to* pray" (Luke 11:1). And pray they did!

As we look into the Book of Acts and several other portions of Scripture, we find the believers mentioned most of the needs that require our prayers.

—For prayer to be successful, the early saints realized they must be in one accord—in unity: 1:14.
—They prayed for the will of the Lord to be done in selecting a replacement for Judas:1:24.
—They had a set time to pray for needs in general: 1:24.
—They prayed as they searched the Scriptures: 6:3.
—They prayed for new converts: 8:15 with John 17:20.
—They prayed for persecuted friends: 12:1–5.
—They prayed for missionaries: 13: 2–4.
—They prayed when suffering in trials: 16:25.

The Principle of Prayer 59

- They prayed one for another: 21:4,5.
- We need to pray for the sick: James 5:14–16.
- Christian workers need our prayers: Matthew 9:18; Colossians 4:3.
- All men, including rulers—those in authority, need our prayers: I Timothy 2:1–3; I Peter 2:17.
- We must pray for Israel: Psalm 122:6; Romans 10:1.
- We must constantly pray for the unsaved. Christ does: Hebrews 7:25,

The Importance of Prayer

It is so important to the heart of God that it is mentioned at least 544 times in the Bible. With it being such an important subject, there are certain conditions in our approach to the Lord.[22]

- We must not regard wickedness in our hearts, for if we do, the Lord will not hear us: Psalm 66:18.
- We must not waver: James 1:6.
- We must heed God's Word: Proverbs 28:9.
- We must not ask amiss: James 4:3. The story is told of a pastor who proposed to a choir member and was turned down. Word spread through the congregation, to the pastor's dismay. The next Sunday a beautiful young widow handed the pastor a note which read, "Ye have not because ye asked a *miss*."
- We must not be proud: Job 35:12,13; James 4:6.
- We must be humble: Psalm 9:12; 10:17
- We must have a forgiving spirit: Mark 11:25; Ephesians 4:32.
- We must hear the cry of the needy: Proverbs 21:13.
- We must have true repentance: Luke 18:13,14.
- We must have faith in Christ and God: I John 5:13–15; Hebrews 11:6.
- We must be godly and righteous: Psalm 32:6.
- We must be obedient: I John 3:22.
- We must be trustful: Psalm 37:4,5.
- Husbands must honor their wives for their prayers to be heard: I Peter 3:7.

Persons Addressed in Prayer

Believers prayed to *God* in behalf of Peter: Acts 12:5.

In Christ's High Priestly prayer, He called upon God as *Holy Father* and *Righteous Father*: John 17:11,25.

Stephen and Corinthian believers called upon *Jesus Christ*: Acts 7:59; I Corinthians 1:2.

We are instructed by Jesus when we pray to the Father to ask in His name (John 14:13; 15:16b). Our request is in the power and under the guidance of the Holy Spirit (Ephesians 2:18). The relation to the Holy Spirit in prayer is brought out in Romans 8:26,27. We are not forbidden to pray to Him. He is the "Lord of the harvest" and we are to pray that He send forth laborers (Matthew 9:38).

The Language of Prayer[23]

With all the modern translations of the Bible bringing the language of the Bible down to man's level, their tone and terms of familiarity used in addressing Deity in public prayer is distasteful at best. It is not wrong to address the Lord—God Almighty— in words that denote personal relationship, but too often it ignores the attributes of a holy and righteous God and the respect and reverence due Him. The Psalmist reminds us of the dignity in prayer: "Let the words of my mouth and the meditation of my heart be acceptable in Thy sight" (Psalm 19:14).

We all know that the King James Version of the Bible is archaic to many of our day, but it does have a dignity about which modern versions do not—a dignity that should be prevalent when *finite* addresses *Infinite*. Although the language of the KJV dates back to 1611, the translators of that day put man on his "level" and God on His "level." Man is referred to as "you" when God speaks to him, or when man speaks to man, but never once when man speaks to God. Someone has counted the number of times when God or men refer to men, and the "you" count is 2,000 times. But when man addresses God, He is shown reverence by using "Thou" and "Thee" more than 2,800 times. What a contrast! Even today if one visits Queen Elizabeth, she is addressed as "Her Majesty" out of respect for her position.

"You" is not found in the dedicatory prayer of the Temple, but God's majesty is recognized by Solomon with the use of the term "Thy" over sixty times (II Chronicles 6). Jesus referred to man as "you" or "him" but not once to His Father. In addressing His prayer to His Father in John 17, He uses "Thine" or "Thou" over forty times. It would do the believer good to remember who God is and to give the respect due Him. In a world weighed down with irreverence, devotion and meditation will go a long way in bringing us back to the place where God and His Son have the preeminence in our thoughts and in our vocabulary as we address each of Them.

Prayer is Reciprocal

This is a Biblical truth that is seldom mentioned. When Christ was dealing with Peter on one occasion, He told him that Satan desired to have him that he might sift him as wheat. Jesus then added, "But I have prayed for you that your faith fail not" (Luke 22:31–34).

When stalks of wheat were brought to the threshing floor and the grain was beaten off the stalks, a man would come with a pitch fork. Scooping up the chaff into the air, it was a sight to behold as the wind would blow it away. All eyes were on the chaff while the "fruit of the wheat" went unnoticed on the threshing floor. Peter had some good points but what the devil wanted to do was magnify his imperfections—his chaff—so that others would point an accusing finger at his hypocrisy.

The Principle of Prayer

When Jesus told Peter He was praying for him that his faith fail not, he was the only one who could answer that prayer. We send *up* our prayers to the Lord and expect Him to send *down* His answers. Often we speak of God as "a prayer hearing and a prayer answering God." Christ, who ever lives to make intercession for us, sends *down* a prayer about our faith not failing and we are the only ones who can send *up* our answer to Him. *Prayer is reciprocal.* I have often wondered what we would do if God didn't answer our prayers any better than we answer His. 0 the need to be obedient to the "Principle of Prayer!"

Did Peter answer this prayer of Christ? No he didn't. He followed Jesus afar off and denied Him three times. But soon after when he saw his blessed Lord, he remembered Christ's prediction and wept bitterly (Luke 22:62).

After this experience of failure to answer Christ's prayer, notice that on the Day of Pentecost and afterward through His life's ministry, he was a living testimony of his faith not failing in answer to Christ's prayer. His experience was a fiery trial of faith. Being used by God to write two Epistles, he sought to encourage believers by making mention if any of our trials and temptations were tried by fire like his that we should be an answer to Christ's prayer and come forth as gold (I Peter 1:6,7; Job 23:10). See "The Principle of Faith," Chapter Seven.

Prayer Suggestions[24]

ITS IMPORTANCE. A narrow gauge prayer is the result of a little conception. When we embrace in our prayers the widest circle of our fellowmen we are the most in tune with the mind of God: I Timothy 2:1.

ITS SERIOUSNESS. God's acquaintance is not made by hasty comers or hurried calls: Jeremiah 29:13.

ITS BASIS. Nothing is beyond the reach of prayer except that which lies outside the will of God. True prayer is not conquering God's unwillingness, but laying hold of His willingness by bringing our prayers in *line* with His will: I John 5:14,15.

ITS GROUND. It is not enough that prayer is offered for a good object. It must come from a heart that is right to be effectual. One may have a good ground for asking yet not be on praying ground himself: James 5:16b.

ITS APPROACH. Unless we pray in the name of Jesus and on the ground of His atonement, our praying is in vain. God honors no drafts where there are no deposits: John 14:14.

ITS PURPOSE. Don't pray for employment "suited" to your abilities, but for power equal to your opportunities. Our need is not for easy lives, but for grace to be stronger Christians in His service: II Corinthians 2:9.

ITS ACTIVITY. Fervent prayer is the "promoter" of activity. It puts one at God's disposal for the carrying out of His part in bringing about the things He desires: Psalm 31:3.

ITS REGULARITY. He who fails to pray, simply because the sun is shining and all seems favorable, will find his power to pray gone when the storm clouds arise: Luke 18:1.

ITS TRAINING. The prayer closet is the one place for the believer to be schooled in waiting upon the Lord. All other training without this proves ineffectual: Matthew 6:5

ITS DEFINITENESS. Many prayers go to the dead-letter office of heaven for want of specific direction. Know of a certainty from the Word of God and by the Spirit what it is that God desires and then ask specifically: Luke 11:9,10.

ITS ESSENTIALNESS. In everything by prayer and supplication, with thanksgiving, make your request known unto God. *This is a command*—[the Principle of Prayer]: Philippians 4:6.

ITS PRACTICE. You may talk much about the philosophy of prayer, but make sure you spend more time in the practice of it than talking about it. I Thessalonians 5:17.

ITS STABILITY. One's ability to get together with God in the place of prayer will be the measure of his ability to get together with God in the place of activity: Psalm 119:117.

ITS DELAYS. Count it a blessing if God delays the answer to your prayer for a time. He may want to enlarge your capacity to receive a greater blessing later: Psalm 37:5.

ITS TESTS. X-rays of the self-life expose failure in the prayer-life. A selfish purpose in prayer always spells defeat. [Sometimes God may grant such an answer but will send leanness to the soul: Psalm 106:15].

ITS SEARCHINGS. Praying will make one lay aside his sinning or else sinning will make him lay aside his praying: Psalm 66:18.

ITS VICTORIES. Victory in life's conflicts is impossible without prayer. Soldiers of the Lord do their very best if they "Cry unto the Lord in battle" (I Chronicles 5:20).

ITS ASSURANCE. We must pray in Christ's name if we expect Him to hear and answer us: John 14:13,14.

SUMMARY

The Challenge of Prayer. Jesus said, "Men ought always to pray and faint not" (Luke 18:1). This command comes from the lips of none other than Jesus Christ to His followers. This verse can be divided into two parts.

1. The word *ought* denotes *must*, which is definitely a command. Not to pray is disobedience. The word *always* denotes "at any and every time when something must be done according to circumstances." This ties in with "Pray without ceasing (I Thessalonians 5:17).

2. The necessity of prayer under any and all circumstances is that if we do not, we will *faint*. The word "faint" here does not mean to pass out. If prayer is not an integral part of our lives, we faint—lack courage, lose hope, grow weary, become fainthearted (discouraged and depressed, dependent upon the flesh), fail to stand up for the Lord when opportunities present themselves, ignore spiritual responsibilities and when this happens, our testimony becomes null and void—powerless, thus making us a stumbling block to others in need.

The Principle of Prayer

The choice is up to us—pray or become faint. Do we become "prayer warriors" and win one battle after another, or do we disobey the "Principle of Prayer" and live in defeat? To neglect prayer is a sin (I Samuel 12:23). Lack of prayer grieves the Lord (Isaiah 43:21,22). Thankfully, prayer is the medium through which God bestows blessings (Matthew 7:11), and is essential to victory over the forces of evil (Ephesians 6:10–18).

Keep in mind the "Secret of prayer is *praying*; It is not so much our knowing *how* to pray, but of *spending time in prayer*. When we shut the door of our prayer closet, this helps us to keep our minds on *why* we are there. The influence of Satan brings things to our minds that distract us from the very purpose of our being there (Matthew 6:6). In our prayer closet we allow the Holy Spirit to get our minds in tune with God's mind so that we can pray according to His will. From there on out, our minds are stayed on Him (Romans 8:26,27; Isaiah 26:3).

> Dear heavenly Father, help me to be a living answer to my Savior's prayers as He prays for my faith to be exercised from day to day. May I watch and pray to Thee with thanksgiving and may the words of my mouth and the meditation of my heart be acceptable in Thy sight, O Lord, my strength and Redeemer. In Jesus' name I pray. Amen.
>
> Luke 22:31; Colossians 4:2; Psalm 19:14

Chapter Eight

THE PRINCIPLE OF FAITH

The writer of Hebrews states that "Without faith it is impossible to please God, for he who comes to Him must believe that He is and that He is a rewarder of them that seek Him" (11:6). The expression, without faith it is impossible to please Him" makes it "The Principle of Faith."

Faith can best be defined as "The title deed of things hoped for, the proof of things which are not being seen" (Hebrews 11:1).[25] Faith can also be defined as "perceiving as fact what is not revealed to the natural senses, the substance of things hoped for, the evidence of things which are not seen." Faith is the opposite of sight. You have heard it said, "I won't believe it 'till I see it." This might sound fine to a skeptic, but who has seen electricity? It may be felt but not seen. God's definition of faith may be confusing to some but we cannot please Him without it. Walking by sight is disobedience, hence the need for *The Principle of Faith* (Romans 3:26,27).

There is a difference between Biblical faith and a current teaching called "Positive Thinking." Positive thinking seeks knowledge to tap the powers of the human mind and to utilize them for confident living. As far as it goes, it might work. But Biblical faith relates to a living God—it makes promises present and real and unseen things visible. Only as we begin to exercise faith in God, His Son and His Word will we obey this Principle and receive what is necessary for a relationship with God and the benefits He provides for our spiritual needs.

The Necessity of Faith

One's *salvation* depends on his faith in the finished work of Christ at Calvary for his sins. Salvation is a gift from God and comes only by grace through *faith*, and not by works (Ephesians 2:8,9). In repentance one has a turn-about-face of his sinful way, while in *faith* he turns to the *cause* of salvation, namely Jesus Christ. Repentance and faith are inseparable. True repentance cannot exist apart from faith. One may repent and not exercise faith in Christ. Paraphrasing John the Baptist's message, "Repent, and prove it by bringing forth evidence to show you have put your faith and trust in Christ's redemptive work (Matthew 3:6–8; I Corinthians 15:3,4).

One's *justification* is derived from faith in Christ for salvation, which makes the saved one righteous. He then has become reconciled to God by faith and is now in a right relationship with Him with nothing between him and God (Romans 3:28; Ephesians 2:15,16).

Faith's Importance After Salvation

Faith gives the believer access to come boldly before God's throne of grace to obtain mercy and find grace in the time of need (Romans 5:2; Hebrews 4:16). *Mercy is God's withholding from us what we rightly deserve and grace is God's giving to us what we don't deserve.*

Faith helps one to stand up for God and before others (II Corinthians 1:24).

Faith strengthens one's character in producing a fruitful life. In our daily walk with the Lord, we can add to our faith virtue, knowledge, temperance, patience, godliness, brotherly kindness, and love as we live and move and have our being in this wicked and perverse world (I Peter 3:5–7; Philippians 2:15).

Faith gives us the peace of God (Romans 5:1; John 16:33).

We have become fellow citizens by faith, having been translated into the kingdom of God's dear Son (Colossians 1:4–14; Philippians 3:20 (New KJV).

Faith has placed us in God's household, making us members of His family (Ephesians 2:18b; John 1:12).

Faith makes us safe and secure on a solid foundation—the solid Rock, Jesus Christ (Ephesians 2:20; Psalm 40:2,3; I Corinthians 3:11).

Faith provides for the Triune God a residence in our bodies. We have become His Temple on earth. God the *Father* walks in us (II Corinthians 6:16; Ephesians 2:22). God the *Son* has His dwelling place within us on this planet (Matthew 28:20b; Ephesians 3:17; Colossians 1:27). God the *Holy Spirit* dwells within the bodies of believers (I Corinthians 3:16; 6:19,20).

Faith enables us to have a good walk with God as we follow in the footsteps of Christ. As we walk with Him, we are being conformed to the image of God's dear Son, and people, as they see us, will take knowledge that we have been with Jesus (II Corinthians 5:7; I Peter 2:21; Acts 4:13).

Faith gives us joy (Philippians 1:25; John 16:33).

Faith positions us as God's workmanship. He has made us what we are so that in Christ we will do good works for Him. We are co-laborers with God (Ephesians 2:10; I Corinthians 3:9).

We are sanctified by faith, *set apart* unto God to perform His will through us (Acts 26:18; I Thessalonians 4:3,7).

Faith prompts prayer (Ephesians 1:15,16).

Faith assures us that God will hear our prayers (James 1:6).

Faith gives us the boldness we need to witness as "Fishers of Men" for Christ's sake (I Timothy 3:13; Matthew 4:19; Proverbs 11:30).

Faith provides for us the fortification, courage and the armor to resist Satan. With such faith we have the wherewithal to be an overcomer, one who is "more than a conqueror through Christ who loves us" (I Peter 5:9; Romans 8:37).

We are to fight the good fight of faith as good soldiers of Christ Jesus (I Timothy 6:12; II Timothy 2:3).

Faith challenges us to be obedient (Romans 16:26).

Faith edifies godliness (I Timothy 1:4).

Faith gives us Christ's mind and strength so that we can do all things through Him for His glory (I Corinthians 2:16; Philippians 4:13).

As we follow faith, we flee evil (I Timothy 6:10,11).

Faith will purify the heart (Acts 15:9).

Faith enables us to face and overcome obstacles (Mark 11:22,23).

Faith works by love (Galatians 5:6). See Chapter Three.

Local sound Churches are founded in faith (Acts 16:5a).

We exercise patience through faith (Romans 14:12).

We become rooted and grounded in the Gospel and love as we exercise faith (Colossians 1:23; Ephesians 3:17).

Faith establishes us and enables us to abound with thanksgiving as we are rooted and built up in Christ (Colossians 2:7).

We can always draw near unto God with a true heart full of assurance of faith (Hebrews 10:21,22).

Faith causes us to abound in everything, which includes knowledge, diligence, love and grace (II Corinthians 8:7).

We are challenged to "keep looking up" to Jesus, the "Author and Finisher" of our faith (Hebrews 12:2).

It is no wonder the writer of Hebrews said that "Without faith it is impossible to please God" (11:6). Our "Faith List" thus far is minimal compared to all the faith verses but enough to let us know the *how* of pleasing God. We are taught that:[26]

> Faith *achieves* (Hebrews 11:4–35a).
> Faith *suffers* (Hebrews 11:35b-38).
> Faith *teaches* us *patience* (James 1:3).
> Faith *rewards* (Hebrews 11:6, 39,40)

The Test or Examination of Faith

In the market of our land, everything as a rule is tested before it reaches the public. Cars, airplanes, medicine' food, etc., go through rigid tests to make sure all function according to the law. It only stands to reason when we consider the importance and necessity of faith in the realm of Christianity, it will face tests. We will be tested to find out if we really believe what we say we believe—to find out if it is pretense or genuine.

Those mentioned in Scripture who had "precious faith", when tried in the fires of testing, came forth more precious than gold (II Peter 1:1; Job 23:10). "Precious" faith brings forth much more fruit to the praise and honor and glory of God. It takes a real Christian to be a real Christian.

One of the best ways to examine any Biblical subject is to go through a Concordance and see how different people, under varied situations and circumstances, responded to this test. It is surprising that the word "faith" is used only *twice* in the Old Testament. Once it is used in reference to the children of Israel becoming a perverse generation and having no faith (Deuteronomy 32:20). The other time is in Habakkuk where it is said "the just shall live by faith" (2:4).

Since the word *faith* is so seldom used in the Old Testament, we can substitute the word *belief* for *faith* in this case. Here are a few who got an "A+" on their "obedience" exam:

> —In Abel's offering a blood sacrifice, which was accepted by the Lord. It became a *justifying faith*, illustrating *worship* (Hebrews 11:4).
> —Enoch's was a *sanctifying faith*, walking in fellowship with God. His walk set him apart unto God. It was a walk of faith that translated him that he should not see death because he had a testimony that pleased God (Genesis 5:22,23; Hebrews 11:5).
> —Noah's was a *separating faith* illustrating *witnessing* before an ungodly people: Hebrews 11:7. Noah's faith is demonstrated in his:[27]
> —Beginning of faith when warned by God
> —Progress of faith in moving with fear
> —Work of faith in preparing the ark
> —Reward of faith with his house being saved
> —Result of faith in the condemnation of the world.
> —Inheritance of faith in his becoming an heir of righteousness.
> —Abraham's belief in God was the means of his:[28]
> —Being declared righteous by faith (Genesis 15:6; Romans 4:3).
> —Living by faith (Romans 4:20,21).
> —Walking by faith (Genesis 12:1–4; Hebrews 11:8).
> —Being tried by faith (Genesis 22:1–13; Hebrews 11:17).
> —Prospering by faith (Hebrews 11:9).
> —Being blessed of God (Hebrews 11:11,12).
> —Looking for and desiring a better home whose "Builder and Maker" is God (Hebrews 11:10,16).
> —His dying in faith (Hebrews 11:13).
> —Joseph's *obedient faith* to the Word of God, illustrating his *morality* when he refused to sin against the Lord in having an affair with another mans wife (Genesis 39:7–9).
> —Moses' *enduring faith*, illustrating his *desire to have heaven's best* rather than to gain the riches of Egypt if he chose to be called the "son of Pharaoh's daughter." He chose rather to suffer afflictions with God's people than to enjoy the pleasures of sin for a season. His eyes were on Christ as seeing Him who is invisible, he had confidence in God's reward. He knew the truth of Christ's warning, "What shall it profit a man if he should gain the whole world but lose his own soul." Like Jacob he put the spiritual before the material (Hebrews 11:23–27 with Mark 8:36).
> —Joshua's *fighting faith*, illustrating his *trust in God* in conquering the Promised Land (Joshua 11:23; 21:43–45).

The Principle of Faith 69

—Rahab's *saving faith*, illustrating her *belief in the spies word* that she and her family would be spared if she would hang a "scarlet thread" out her window when the Israelites invaded Jericho. In protecting the spies, she acknowledged her belief in Israel's God. Having been told to hang the "scarlet thread" out the window when Israel entered for conquest, her faith told her to hang it out *then*. Not knowing when the invasion would take place, she knew she would be ready at a moment's notice (Joshua 1–21). Her faith paid off great dividends in the saving of her and her whole family when the walls of Jericho came a'tumbling down (Joshua 6:21–25).

The scarlet (red) thread could well be a type of blood, a strong resemblance to the ordinance of the Passover. The binding of this thread by Rahab answers to the blood sprinkled on the door posts. Her house was the only safe place in Jericho, and just as none of the Israelites were to go out of their house till the death angel passed over, none of Rahab's family was to leave her house until Joshua dealt a death blow to Jericho. Her house had become a house of peace which can only come when blood is applied (Hebrews 11:31).

—David's *victorious faith*, illustrating his *boldness* as a lad to fight against Goliath, a giant over nine feet tall, with only an insignificant small sling stone (I Samuel 17:4,48:51). David's brothers tried to persuade him to go home, that Goliath was too big to defeat. But David's faith in God was so strong he knew Goliath was too big to miss!

—Elijah's *bold faith*, illustrating his *willingness to stand alone* against 450 prophets of Baal and 400 prophets of the groves, a ratio of 850 to one, to prove that his God was the one *true* God (I Kings 18:17–19). As a pastor, I was approached by a member who requested prayer that he might get a job where there were Christians, saying he was fed up being abused daily by fellow workers who were rank unbelievers. Replying that I could offer no prayer as requested, I reminded him that God placed him in his employment to be a witness to these people. Working with believers is easier, but he soon realized he had opportunities to witness and possibly lead some to the Lord. We then prayed for God to use him and after several months some had trusted in Christ. God always knows how to engineer circumstances to accomplish His purposes.

—Jeremiah's *persistent faith*, illustrating his *faithful trust* in the Word of God (20:7–14).

—Hezekiah's *praying faith*, illustrating his *dependence* upon the Lord to defeat the Assyrian king, Sennacherib, to spare Jerusalem (II Kings (8:14,17; 19:14–20,32–31).

The eleventh Chapter of Hebrews, in giving us a summary of many Old Testament saints of their *living faith*, illustrating their *trust in the Lord* for a future home in glory with Him (Hebrews 11:32–40).

In our approach of the subject of *faith* in the New Testament, we find this word is used at least 258 times compared to only two in the Old Testament. Its greater use shows the importance of man having a personal relationship with God, which is spiritual. The word *believe* is often used for faith, such as when the Apostle John told his hearers they could become a child of God by *receiving* and *believing* on Jesus Christ (John 1:12). The same is implied when Jesus quoted John 3:16 to Nicodemus. This truth is also brought out in the Acts and by the Apostles in the Epistles. Peter, on the Day of Pentecost, said in effect if you *believe* what I have preached, "Repent, prove it by renouncing your Judaism by being baptized, and you will receive the promise of the Father, the gift of the Holy Spirit." Almost 3,000 did and they were added to the Church. Peter's *one* sermon resulted in almost 3,000 being saved (Acts 2:37–41). Today, it seems like it takes 3,000 sermons to produce one convert! We notice also that Paul used the word *believe* when he told the Philippian jailor to "believe on the Lord Jesus Christ," which he, along with his family did, and they all experienced salvation by faith (Acts:16:31–34).

At times, faith has a physical use but it always leads to the spiritual. During the ministry of Christ, faith was the means of healing multitudes of people of their diseases (sicknesses), lameness, deafness, blindness, and even on a few occasions Jesus raised some from the dead (Matthew 9:22; Luke 7:22). Miracles of healing were performed by some Apostles after Christ's ministry (Acts 3:2–9; 5:12–15; 14:9). In each instance of physical healing, it was to drive home a need to exercise faith in Christ for their soul's need.

Faith's ultimate use is for one's salvation and godly living to prove that their faith is real. Being saved through faith, and not by our works, we immediately become God's workmanship (Ephesians 2:8–10). The salvation God wrought in our hearts is to be worked out or demonstrated by us daily, showing forth the praises of Him who has called us out of darkness into His marvelous light (Philippians 2:12; I Peter 2:9).

Sight Versus Faith

We have seen illustrations of faith established by various characters in the Old Testament, and numerous ones are mentioned in the New. Their examples are wonderful challenges for believers of our day. In Paul's first letter to the Corinthians he mentions the evil behavior of many Israelites due to their disobedience. Their actions showed they were walking by sight and not by faith. Paul warns us not to follow their examples, that their misbehavior was recorded for us that we might not follow their example, that they were recorded for our admonition (10:5–11). Paul hastens to add that we should take heed lest we fall prey to walking by sight and not by faith. We are still in the flesh, but when temptation comes, God always provides a way of escape that we may be able to bear it (vss. 12,13). If only Israel had obeyed "The Principle of Faith."

We can actually go back to the Garden of Eden with Adam and Eve and lead up to the children of Israel to note their "sight walk."

Eve *saw* the beautiful fruit, *desired* to have it, and then *took* it. She not only disobeyed God but enticed Adam to eat the forbidden fruit, which brought sin to the whole human race (Genesis 3:6; Romans 5:12).

Lot *saw* the fertile plains of Jordan, *desired* them and *took* them for monetary value, which caused him to compromise with the Sodomites and lose his testimony with the Lord and his family (Genesis 13:10,11; 19:1–14).

The tribes of Reuben, Gad and half-Manasseh *saw* the fertile farm lands east of Jordan and *desired* them, and *took* them, forfeiting the right of their inheritance in the Promised Land. As a result they were the first to be taken into captivity by the Assyrians (I Chronicles 5:26).

Achan *saw* the gold and silver vessels of Jericho that were consecrated unto the Lord, *desired* them and *took* them. Although he confessed his sin God's judgment fell upon him and his family (Joshua 6:19; 7:18–26).

When the twelve spied out the land of Canaan, ten *saw* the power of the nations and *desired* not to enter their inheritance. They *took* matters in their own hands by refusimg to exercise faith in God's promise to go before them to possess it. Joshua records that the ten spies brought back an evil report, that the inhabitants were stronger than they, that they were but grasshoppers in the sight of the inhabitants who were giants, and that they had no defense against the walled cities. Joshua and Caleb obeyed God in walking by faith and said, "Let us go up now and possess it, for we will defeat them. They are prey for us and their defense is departed from them. The Lord is with us, fear them not" (Numbers 13:30; 14:7–9). The people refused the report of the "faith spies," demanded their death, and were sentenced by God to forty years of wilderness wandering. See Hebrews 3:8,9. One thing learned in this *incident—the majority is not always right*.

After Israel received her inheritance in the Promised land, many Israelites did not follow the Lord. Prior to Joshua's death the people promised Joshua they would follow the Lord (Joshua 24:16–18). After Joshua's death, a generation rose up who did not know the Lord and they began to worship Baal, the idol of the Canaaanites (Judges 2:11,12; 3:5–7). Desiring freedom under the rule of self-government, they dethroned God and chose a "man" king (I Samuel 8:19,20). For about the next 500 years the vast number of Israelites lived in idolatry. How thankful we can be for the faithful remnant who preserved the lineage through which Jesus would come (Isaiah 1:9).

King David was said to be a man "after God's own heart" (Acts 13:22) yet he put aside his faith in the Lord, ignored Him and His commandment when he *saw* Bathsheba, *desired* her and *took* her (II Samuel 11; 12:9,10).

Although he repented, confessed his sin and was forgiven, 'till his dying day he reaped what he had sown (Psalm 51; 32:1–5 with II Samuel 12:10).

Peter had faith to believe he could walk on water when Christ told him to come to Him. After a few steps, he *saw* boisterous winds, took his eyes off the Lord and began to sink. Christ rescued him when he cried for help, but chastised him by saying, "0 you of little faith, why did you doubt" (Matthew 14:26–31).

The faith of Demas turned to sight when he forsook the things of the Lord for the pleasures of sin the world offered (II Timothy 4:10).

In the case of "Doubting Thomas," his experience was quite the reverse He said he wouldn't believe that Christ had been raised from the grave 'till he saw him. Upon seeing Jesus, he didn't even have to feel His hands and side, his sight turned to faith as he exclaimed, "My Lord and my God'" (John 20:24–29).

The illustrations of those whose faith turned into sight should be reminders to us to pass the test when our faith is tested by a fiery trial. They realized no strange thing had happened to them (I Peter 4:12). We are admonished to examine ourselves to see if we truly are in the faith and to prove it (II Corinthians 13:5). We need to say what the Apostles said to Jesus, "Lord, *increase* our faith" (Luke 17:5). No matter how much faith we think we have, we need to keep putting it into practice lest we fall. Our Christian experience must be a constant growth in grace and knowledge of our Lord and Savior Jesus Christ (II Peter 3:18). When we lack the faith necessary for any situation, we—

> Doubt the Scripture that would help to deliver us and give victory.
> Go around in circles like Israel did in her wilderness wanderings and like Samson did when he had to turn the grindstone after getting a haircut in the devil's barbershop.
> Might experience hard times like Job (1:13–2:10).
> Become prejudiced like Jonah and run from the Lord (Jonah 1:1–3).
> Consider the material over the spiritual like the rich young ruler Matthew 19:16–22).
> Rebel against the Lord and question His dealings with us, like Joshua did when he found sin in the camp (7:1,5–9).
> Become discouraged and fail to "get up and go" by having our own little "pity party" like Elijah and Jonah did (I Kings 18:3,4; Jonah 4:1–3).
> Sin, because anything that is not of faith is sin (Romans 14:23b).

Faith Without Works

When Martin Luther discovered the truth that "the just shall live by faith" and not by the works of tradition, he ruled that the Book of James was not a part of inspired Scripture because it taught that "faith without works is dead" (Habakkuk 2:4; Romans 1:17; James 2:26). He soon learned that if a man really has faith to live the Christian life, it will be shown by the works (deeds) he performs for his Savior. If our faith is not productive, we cannot trust God for[29]

> *Help* if we are not making any effort.
> *Strength* if we have strength and are not using it.
> *Guidance* if we are not following His leading.
> *Prosperity* if we have proved we cannot be trusted with it.
> *Truth* when we will not act upon what we already know.
> *Forgiveness* if we will not forgive someone else.
> *Mercy* if we intend to commit the same sin again.
> *Faith* if we neglect His Word.

When lack of faith befalls us and we are

> *Impatient*, sit down quietly wth Job.
> *Strongheaded*, go and see Cain.

Weakkneed, go with Elijah to Mount Carmel.
Compromising, read Daniel.
Without a song, sing with David as he plays his harp.
Cold to the things of God, fellowship with the beloved disciple, John.
About ready to *give up*, listen to Jeremiah.
Feeling *forgotten*, visit Joseph in Egypt.
Down in the dumps, look to Jesus the Author and Finisher of our faith.
Becoming lazy, sign up with James.
Losing sight of the future, climb the stairs of the book of
Revelation and get a glimpse of our heavenly Jerusalem (Chapters 21,22).
If your faith is weak and you are[30]
Distressed, don't look within. *Defeated*, don't look back.
Distracted, don't look around.
Dismayed, don't look ahead.
Disappointed, don't look to man.
Desirous to be delivered, look to Christ.
Anxious to be *Delighted*, look up.

One of the best ways we can encourage ourselves is to look at some believers like Stephen and Barnabas who were full of faith and power (Acts 6:5; 11:22–24). Many faithful workers in the faith who helped Paul, Peter and John (Paul especially) are mentioned in the latter part of Romans and other Epistles. Make a habit of reading Hebrews Eleven occasionally.

SUMMARY

As we examine our study of faith in this chapter, the best way to keep "The Principle of Faith" is to:

Examine ourselves to see if we are in the faith, to prove it before others as we have faith *with* works (II Corinthians 13:5; James 2:20).

Study the Scriptures to show ourselves approved unto God. This is God's solution for our having and increasing our faith, for faith comes by hearing the Word of God (II Timothy 2:15; Romans 10:17).

Hold fast the profession of our faith without wavering (Hebrews 10:23).

Keep the faith to fight the good fight of faith so we can finish our course (II Timothy 4:7).

Continue in the faith (Acts 14:22).

Trust God to provide a way of escape when we are tempted and give us victory as we overcome Satan's tactics (I Corinthians 10:13; I John 5:4b).

Face any and all obstacles through Christ's strength which confront us by having faith in God (Mark 11:22,23).

Be faithful witnesses by taking the advice of Paul to Philemon and communicate—share the Gospel with others (Philemon 1:6; Matthew 10:32,33).

In reference to Christ's return for His own, he asked the question, "When I come will I find faith?" (Luke 18:8). For Him to find faith in us we must be an answer to His prayer, "I have prayed for you that your faith fail not" (Luke 22:31,32). See "Prayer is Reciprocal" in Chapter Seven. We must constantly ask Him to "increase our faith" so that He will never say to us, "O you of little faith" (Luke 12:28b). True faith proves what we say is what we believe with all our heart. True faith causes us to believe every word of God. *He said it, I believe it, and that settles it!*

Faith is so important, so near to the heart of God, that every redeemed child of His is duty bound to follow "The Principle of Faith" in contending or striving to present the same faith which was first delivered unto the saints (Jude 3). Jude tells us *how* we are to contend for or share the faith—

Build ourselves up in the faith through the Word of God (vs. 20a with Romans 10:17).

Pray in the Holy Spirit (vs. 20b with Romans 8:26,27).

Keep yourselves in the love of God (vs. 21a with Mark 12:30,31).

Looking for Christ's return (vs. 21b with I John 2:28).

Being a soul winner (22,23a with Proverbs 11:30; Daniel 12:3). As the redeemed ones of God, we are to say so (Psalm 107:2; Acts 1:8).

Live a separated life from the world (vs. 23b with Romans 12:1,2).

Faith's goal is for one to be saved and to live godly to prove that their faith is real. Being saved by grace though faith and not by our works, we immediately become God's workmanship (worker; servant: Ephesians 2:8–10). The salvation God has wrought in our hearts is to be *worked* out and *demonstrated* by us to a lost and dying world, showing forth the praises of Him who has called us out of darkness into His marvelous light (I Peter 2:9).

By our giving all diligence to what Scripture has taught us about our exhibiting faith, we are told in Second Peter 1:5,6 that we can best demonstrate it by adding to our faith—

>   *Virtue*—moral worth, strength. Add to *Virtue*
>   *Knowledge*—of the Scripture. Add to *Knowledge*
>   *Temperance*—self-control. Add to *Self-control*
>   *Patience*—enduring difficulties. *Add. to Patience*
>   *Godliness*—revealing Christ in us. Add to *Godliness*
>   *Brotherly kindness*—unselfish deeds. Add to *Kindness*
>   *Love*—first toward God and then to others.

Faith is a powerful tool that when exercised according to the will of God, it can handle any situation that confronts us, and at the same time it gives us the will to keep forging ahead as a good soldier of Christ, fighting the good fight of faith so that we might finish our course.

A Prayer Thought

Lord, I fully realize You have made every provision for all Your children to utilize under all circumstances. Help me to know that faith is dead to doubts, ignorant of discouragements, blind to impossibilities and knows nothing but success.

Also, please help me so that when Christ comes He will find in me the faith He expects to find among those who have dared to be faithful. May my faith enable others to notice that I have been with Jesus. In His name I pray, Amen.
(Luke 18:8; Romans 14:23b; Hebrews 11:6)

Chapter Nine

THE PRINCIPLE OF THE HARVEST

The bulk of the laws in Scripture apply to God's children, but "The Principle of the Harvest" applies to both sinner and saint alike. It states: "Be not deceived, God is not mocked, for whatsoever a man soweth, that shall he also reap" (Galatians 6:7). The Apostle Paul elaborates on this law in verse eight by telling the sinner what he will reap if he sows to his flesh (worldly sinful ways) and what the Christian will reap by sowing to the Spirit. The sinner reaps corruption, the exact opposite of what the believer reaps, which is a Christless eternity as opposed to a believer reaping eternal life in Christ.

Several principles are noted in "The Principle of the Harvest," one of which is *cause and effect*. We cannot do something (*cause*) and think for one moment there will be no effect or that the *something* ends there. We cannot fool God for He cannot be mocked. In fact, we may think we are fooling ourselves but the reaping process will prove us wrong every time. No sowing is done without reaping, nor is any reaping done without sowing. Whatever we sow, it was done by choice. When a farmer chooses to plant corn he expects to reap corn. If he plants watermelon seeds, he does not expect lemons. Whatever we sow, *that* shall we also reap, and our sowing is based on our decision.

Sowing to the Flesh

We know that when a seed is planted in the ground, takes root, grows properly and blossoms forth, that it multiplies itself. It brings forth an increase *after* its kind. Sowing to the flesh means sowing seeds which are produced by the sinner's human, sinful nature. When these seeds are sown, in God's sight they are unacceptable unto Him and He classifies them as "corruption," which produces a decaying harvest followed by death.

What are some of the things which are sown by the flesh, this nature which has not been touched by God's redeeming grace? The works of the flesh are immorality, impurity, indecency, idolatry, sorcery, strife, jealousy, hatred, anger, selfishness, dissention, envy, heresies, drunkenness, murders (Galatians 5:19–21). When man's sinful nature sows such, a multiple harvest of the same kind is reaped, and the ultimate end is that none of the sowers will inherit the kingdom of God (I Corinthians 6:9–11).

Sow a little selfishness, reap a heart full of greed. Sow a small lie, reap a dishonest character. Sow a resentful thought, reap a bitter spirit. Sow a polite curse, reap a stream of profanity. Sow an impure thought, reap an immoral life. Sow a little intemperance, reap drunkenness. Sow anger, reap hatred. Sow coveting, reap theft. Sow bitterness, reap hate.

Not only is there reaping when conducted by individuals, but sowing to the flesh is also done by groups. From year to year and from generation to generation the reaping goes on. We sow lawlessness and we reap crime. We sow liberal parents and reap broken homes and deliquent children. We sow modernism in many Churches and reap unbelief and liberalism.

The harvest we are now reaping is bad enough. The family is crumbling and divorces are rising. Men and women are living together without marriage, and same sex people are marrying and adopting children. Human sacrifice has become legal in the form of abortion. Alcohol and dope are on the increase, especially among our youth. The average age of criminals is decreasing. Sex disease is running rampant. So many politicians are dishonest and the public in general has taken the attitude, "So what, who cares." This attitude is taken because they think our government is running smoothly and the country is prospering, no matter what the leadership does. So many today are blind to the harvest.

With materialism being what it is, what about our next generation? Scripture says "righteousness exalts a nation, but sin is a reproach to any people" (Proverbs 14:34). Our country has been sowing to the flesh for a goodly number of years, and I shudder to think what is next for America. I am reminded of the warning Jesus gave mothers with small children about an impending troublesome time, knowing they would be caught up in reaping what those before them had sown (Luke 21:23).

In addition to individual and group sowers, there are nations that have sown bad seeds and have reaped a devastating harvest. Taking a look at history, ancient nations, because of their leaders desire for power they have come and gone, such as the ancient Assyrians, Persians, Egyptians, Greeks, And we all remember the saying "The rise and fall of the Roman Empire." Even as we look at two World Wars, Western materialism sown in Japan that resulted in Pearl Harbor, the sowing of the atom bomb and the harvest of the nuclear bomb, the Korean and Vietnam wars, the oppression of Communism and the genocide being practiced by some dictators in European countries. Today politics at home and abroad have resulted in millions of innocent people having to reap what others have sown. God help us all, especially as we see America headed in the direction of the harvest of "history repeats itself." How true the statement that "sowing to the flesh will reap corruption."

All that we have mentioned which refers to "sowing to the flesh, " things look mighty bleak. Sowing to the flesh reaps destruction, decay, and ultimately death. However, there is an out for any sinner, regardless of what his harvest might be, and Christ is able to save unto the uttermost all who come unto God by Him.

God is not willing that any should perish but that all should repent and trust Christ as their Savior. His finished work at Calvary has made it possible for one to be delivered from a harvest of corruption. God can lift any sinner out of the miry clay of sin when he is willing to "let go of self and let God take over." God then will put him in a position whereby he might begin—

Sowing to the Spirit

Having considered the doom of those who continue to sow to the flesh, which will bring a harvest of a *Christ less* eternity, those who sow to the Spirit will reap eternal life. Reaping eternal life not only implies our living forever, it has to do with our living in such a way that we make sure we sow that which has been ordained by God. What are the things that we can sow to the Spirit? They are listed in Galatians 5:22,23; *love, joy, peace, longsuffering/patience, gentleness/meekness, goodness/virtue, faithfulness,* and *self-control.* Paul adds this statement to this list of rich fruits, "Against such there is no law." This statement sounds like a contradiction since sowing such is a law. The thought is that when believers are living in and walking by the Holy Spirit in exhibiting this fruit, there cannot be any condemnation of any external law that would prohibit one from bearing any of the fruit of the Spirit. We can thank God for a life that can be tilled and watered by the Holy Spirit to bear this fruit.

We can also thank God that He hasn't abandoned His world. Although the harvest of man's sin is running wild, in His sovereign grace He checks and restrains it by means of another harvest—the harvest of the Holy Spirit. If it were not for His doing this our times would be far worse than they are. We cannot begin to imagine how wicked and depraved people would be, what limitless corruption and degradation would prevail if it were not for the Spirit's harvest, which benefits all mankind. It gives God's blessings as it works in opposition to the harvest of the flesh.

As wonderful as the harvest of the Spirit is, it doesn't work in the lives of all. It is limited to those who have been born again and have the Holy Spirit within them through faith in Jesus Christ. Only these have the seed of a new, resurrected life and they alone are the only ones who can sow to the Spirit. A little sowing of Scripture in their hearts and they begin to reap a harvest of growth in grace and knowledge of God in their lives. And this leads to a willingness to start sowing the seeds of:

Love. This is what fulfills all of the law, as Christ mentioned (Matthew 22:37–42). As we sow faith, this works love and gives a harvest of an intense desire to please God as we make a total sacrifice of self unto Him (Galatians 5:6b). See Chapter on Love.

Joy. This seed is a result of having drawn water out of the wells of God's salvation (Psalm 12:3; 21:1). When God sowed the seed of salvation on Calvary's cross, it offered a harvest of joy that is unspeakable and full of glory (I Peter 1:8).

A harvest of joy produces a harvest of joy in the heart of God as He sees His children walk in truth (III John 4). In joy we reap a song and as we serve the Lord with gladness we make a joyful noise unto Him as we sing in His presence (Psalm 40:2,3; Psalm 100:1,2). We even shout for joy because we have put our trust in Him (Psalm 5:11).

Peace. This seed came as a result of our justification when we exercised faith in Christ (Romans 5:1). God said there is no peace to the wicked, which is a result of his sowing to the flesh (Isaiah 57:20,21). But oh the peace which one possesses when all his troublesome sins are forgiven. What a blessing it is to have sown good seeds all day long and can lie down at night in peace and sleep (Psalm 4:8). Christians might have tribulation in the world, but because Christ is our harvest of peace, we can overcome the world (John 16:33). By keeping our hearts and minds focused on Christ, we can sow a life of prayer and reap a peace that passes all understanding (Philippians 4:6,7).

Longsuffering. This is a seed which must produce a harvest of *patience* under any and all circumstances. We are admonished to "forebear one another in love" (Ephesians 4:2). In our daily routine as a Christian, there are some irritating situations in which we might be tempted to "blow off some steam" and let someone have a piece of our mind. In longsuffering we must make our words sweet so that when we have to "eat them," they will satisfy our sweet tooth! Sowing "longsuffering" helps us to reap a harvest of "bearing one another's burdens," lending a helping hand when needed. This involves "loving our neighbors as we love ourselves, esteeming others better than self" (Philippians 2:3). Longsuffering also applies to situations which confront us personally. The Christian life is not a bed of roses, and there are fiery trials that come our way from time to time. If we sow this seed properly, our harvest will enable us to bear all the difficulties of life without murmuring. We are taught that all things are of God (II Corinthians 5:18), *all* things are for our sake (II Corinthians 4:15), and *all* things work together for our good (Romans 8:28). This being true, come what may, by our submitting cheerfully to every *all*, we reap a satisfactory harvest in every occurence without asking why or complaining.

Gentleness. This involves our sowing good behavior toward others so that we will reap a harvest of their good behavior toward us (Luke 6:31). Gentleness is closely associated with the word *meekness.* Weakness is nowhere involved but it involves a humble heart with a willingness to forebear and be gentle in our treatment of others. Meekness revolves around, not insisting on the "letter of the law" but the "letter of the Spirit." Gentleness produces a life that is not controlled by self, but one that is, in all humility, dedicated to permitting the life of Christ to be manifested in us. This comes about only by the implanted Word of God in our hearts. This is what gives the Christians hope (I Peter 1:21; 3:15).

Goodness. Throughout Scripture, this word carries with it the thought of *virtue.* The combined words of goodness and virtue speak of power, kindness, and the exercise of faith. They all denote honor and influence. Do we have enough power of the Holy Spirit to influence others in the things of God? Have you been kindly affectioned one to another with brotherly love, in honor preferring one an-

The Principle of the Harvest

other lately (Romans 12:10)? In the exercising of our faith do we always keep in mind that without faith it is impossible to please God, and that anything that is not of faith is sin (Hebrews 11:6; Romans 14:23b)?

To encourage us in our sowing goodness and virtue, God has promised us a wonderful harvest in the ages to come. It is that of exceeding riches of His grace in His kindness toward us in Jesus Christ (Ephesians 2:7). This harvest is a result of our "putting on a heart of compassion, kindness, humility, meekness, longsuffering, gentleness and patience, forbearing one another and forgiving one another" (Colossians 3:12; Ephesians 4:32).

Faithfulness. Paul sums up faithfulness twice by saying, "By the grace of God I am what I am, and His grace was not bestowed upon me in vain. I labored more abundantly than all my fellow laborers, yet not I but the grace of God with me" (II Corinthians 15:10). About ready to die, he gave us this testimony: "I have fought a good fight, I have finished my course, I have kept the faith" (II Timothy 4:7,8). Paul showed faithfulness and he reaped a crown of righteousness. "Faithfulness is punctuality in performing God's promises, the conscientious carefulness in preserving what He has committed to our trust."[31] If we are faithful until our dying day, we will reap a crown of life (Revelation 2:10). Loyalty to our heavenly Father will give us this harvest.

Self-control, or temperance. Paul gives us a good example regarding this subject when he mentioned the rigid self-control practiced by athletes as they sought to win a prize. "Everyone who competes in games exercises self-control in all things" (I Corinthians 9:25). Believers are still housed in an earthly body and we are to control it and its appetites and passions. We must take hold of our being crucified with Christ and having been raised to walk in newness of life. The right use of this walk demands discipline in all circumstances so that we might sow the mind of Christ—not ours—to think straight and obey the Spirit as He seeks to order our steps in the Word of God so that no passion or fleshly appetites will have any control upon our lives (I Corinthians 2:16; Psalm 119:133). Unless we yield to the Lord daily, we will handle the Word of God deceitfully but by sowing seeds of temperance or self-control, we are assured of reaping an incorruptible crown. Paul implied the reason he would not become a slave to his bodily passions was so that when he preached to others, they would know that he was preaching the truth (I Corinthians 9:25–27). Whatever we eat or drink, or whatever we do, do all to the glory of God (I Corinthians 10:31).

In addition to the fruit of the Spirit that we can sow, there are many other seeds that produce a spiritual healthy harvest for the redeemed of the Lord. As we sow seeds of *purity* we can reap an increasing holiness of heart and life as we set an example before others (I Timothy 4:12). Sowing *hope* produces confidence and security (Job 11:18). From the seed of patience comes rest of soul (Psalm 37:7). As we sow *yieldness* to all that God permits to come our way, we reap a growth in the image of God's dear Son (Romans 8:28,29).

"All Bible fruits belong to a harvest of eternal life, the life which transcends all physical existence, the life which is beyond earth and time, is the life whose essence is fellowship with God."[32]

Biblical Examples of Sowing and Reaping

Our hearts can always be challenged by a study of Biblical characters. Their "ups and downs" help to teach us what to sow and what not to sow. In the few mentioned we will see that the harvest is always larger than the seed, as is true in the natural.

Cain sowed a horrible seed in killing his brother and reaped his losing the presence of God (Genesis 4:8–16). He is a reminder to all who disobey the Lord that God had pronounced a "woe" upon them (Jude 11). Abel was an obedient child in sowing a sacrifice acceptable unto God, and his harvest has continued—"he being dead, yet speaks today" (Hebrews 11:4).

Abraham sowed a seed of impatience in bearing a son named Ishmael by his handmaid, Hagar, instead of waiting on God to fulfill His promise of a seed through his wife, Sarah (Genesis 16:1–4,11,12). The harvest of Ishmael is seen in his descendants down through the centuries until our time and are called the Arabs. They claim Abraham is their father through Ishmael and are the bitter enemies of the Hebrews. When Abraham sowed a seed of faith, his son Isaac was the seed of promise and the ultimate harvest was the birth of God's only begotten Son, the Lord Jesus Christ (Genesis 17:19; 21:3–10).

When the spies viewed Jericho, Rahab helped them escape from Jericho's king. Because of her belief in Israel's God, she was promised deliverance when Israel invaded the land. In sowing her seed of faith by hanging out the scarlet thread which assured her of deliverance, she reaped a harvest of her whole family being saved (Joshua 2:18; 6:22,23).

David was known as a man after God's own heart (Acts 13:22). He was a brave warrior in leading Israel to victory over several nations. His actions convinced the people of his love for the Lord. One day he lost self-control and committed adultery and had the husband of the woman killed. In sowing these seeds of willful sin, he reaped a harvest of the enemies of the Lord blaspheming and the child of Bathsheba dying. As long as David was alive, the reaping of God's "sword" never did depart from his household (II Samuel 11,12). Yet God forgave him upon His confession and David was used of God to give us a harvest of seventy three of the 150 Psalms. The Twenty Third, in particular, has been an encouragement and a rich blessing to saints down through the centuries.

We need only to read the Eleventh Chapter of Hebrews to learn what so many of the Old Testament saints sowed and the harvest of blessings that became theirs as they obeyed the Lord, even though it cost many their lives. But their sowing assured them of a harvest to be in the City whose Builder and Maker is God.

On a number of occasions we see Peter sowing sarcastic remarks and even denying Christ three times, reaping a harvest of bitter tears and rebuke at times. But on the Day of Pentecost and during the period of the Acts, we see him sowing the Word of God and the reaping of thousands of souls being won to Christ. As an unlearned fisherman, God inspired him to write two Epistles, the seeds of which have helped believers to have a harvest of victory in many circumstances of life, lessons he himself learned by sowing the right seeds.

The Principle of the Harvest 83

The Prodigal son sowed a life of waste and the harvest brought him so low he had to eat with pigs. Yet in repentance, he sowed a willingness to humble himself before the Lord and he reaped a harvest of being welcomed back into full fellowship with his father (Luke 15:11–24). What a great lesson for many teen-agers in our land today.

The visit of Jesus to the house of Mary and Martha provides a good lesson for us in the matter of sowing and reaping. You would think His visit into their home would have caused both to give Him a royal welcome. Martha was a typical hostess—anxious to go to the kitchen to prepare a bit of refreshment. Mary wanted to sit at the feet of Jesus and learn more of Him and the purpose of His coming to this earth.

Martha was cumbered about with minor details. She was thinking more of sowing a seed that would get a pat on the back from Christ for tasty earthly food and she reaped the loss of deep fellowship with the One who was the Bread of Life.

Mary sowed time out from her schedule of daily routine to welcome this unexpected Guest and reaped a "good part" with a dear Friend while Martha was in the kitchen burdened about with much service. Mary was reaping much unspeakable joy and rich fellowship with Jesus. I wonder what I would do if I received a personal visit from Jesus like these sisters did. What would you do:

If Jesus Came to Your House?[33]

If Jesus came to your house to spend a day or two—
If He came unexpectedly, I wonder what you'd do?
Oh, I know you'd give Him your nicest room—this honored Guest,
And all the food you'd serve to Him would be the very best;
And you would keep assuring Him you're glad to have Him there,
That serving Him in your home is joy beyond compare.

But, when you saw Him coming, would you meet Him at the door
With arms outstretched in welcome to your Heavenly Visitor?
Or would you have to change your clothes before you let Him in
Or hide some magazines and put the Bible where they'd been?
Would you turn off the television and hope He hadn't heard
And wish you hadn't uttered that loud, hasty word?

Would you hide your worldly music and put some hymn books out?
Could you let Jesus walk right in, or would you rush about?
And I wonder—if the Savior spent a day or two with you,
Would you go right on doing the things you always do?
Would you go right on saying the things you always say?
Would life for you continue as it does from day to day?

Would your family conversation keep up its usual pace
And would you find it hard each meal to say a table grace?

Would you sing the songs you always sing and read the books you read
And let Him know the things on which your mind and spirit feed?
Would you take Jesus with you everywhere you'd planned to go
Or would you, maybe, change your plans for just a day?

Would you be glad to have Him meet your closest friends
Or would you hope they'd stay away till His visit ends?
Would you be glad to have His stay forever on and on
Or would you sigh with great relief when He at last was gone?
It might be interesting to know the things that you would do
If Jesus Christ in Person came to spend some time with you?

This poem demands a lot of soul-searching. We take so many things for granted and only as the Holy Spirit checks up on us do we take the necessary inventory to determine whether we are sowing to the flesh or to the Spirit. Soul-searching should be a daily routine so that we might constantly sow in the Spirit and reap those things which are God pleasing and God honoring.

CONCLUSION

Having gone through portions of Scripture to learn what believers in particular are to sow, we can summarize our study by considering two parables Jesus taught about a harvest.

1. The parable of sowing the "seed of the Word of God" (Mark 4:1–20). Prior to one's being lifted out of the miry clay of sin, seeds of corruption were sown to the flesh. Coming to Christ and receiving the Holy Spirit, the heart was prepared to partake of God's Word, for this "seed" to be sown to have a productive harvest of fruit unto the Lord. Having been ordained to go and bring forth good fruit, this puts us in a position whereby we can ask our heavenly Father what is needed to have a good harvest and are given the assurance it will come to pass (John 15:16). Upon being informed of our need, as we obey we *abide* or *continue* sowing that which will produce a harvest of *much* fruit (John 15:5).

2. The parable of the "harvest of tares and wheat" (Matthew 13:24–30). He said there are two harvests growing side by side in the field of this world, one of tares or weeds and one of wheat. Jesus said "Let both grow together unto the harvest and in the time of harvest I will say to the reapers, gather up first the tares, [the unbelievers who sowed to the flesh] and burn them (vs. 30).

Christ then refers to the harvest of wheat—a gathering of believers in Christ. This is a gathering of God's wheat not on this side of the grave but on the other side—our gathering unto eternal life. Although some believers had produced fruits of the flesh, at the Judgment Seat of Christ this will be settled, but all on God's threshing floor are gathered into God's granaries of heaven. They have reaped a harvest of eternal life in all its beauty and joy, there to be with their Savior for forever and forever.

The Principle of the Harvest

A question must be asked of someone who might be reading this and as of now have not trusted in Christ as their Savior. You are living apart from God and are sowing to your flesh, heedless of His saving grace. Your ultimate harvest will be corruption, eternal death unless you repent of your sins and by faith trust Christ. Then your sowing will be to the Spirit and you will join all the redeemed of all ages in God's heavenly grainery—heaven *itself*!

A Prayer Thought

Dear Lord, as I look back over my life prior to my being saved and recall the "wild oats" I sowed, I am thankful for Your grace that lifted me out of the miry clay of sin and gave me Your Spirit so that I can sow the "Seeds" of Your Word in my heart. Help me to constantly sow those seeds to the Spirit so that when I reap eternal life in glory, I will have an abundant harvest of fruit to lay at the feet of Jesus in appreciation for all He did for me. In His name I pray. Amen. (Psalm 119:10,11; 104–106)

Chapter Ten

THE PRINCIPLE OF SEPARATION

There are two groups of human beings on planet earth, those who are personally acquainted with Jesus Christ called "Christians" and the unsaved whose father is Satan (Galatians 3:26; John 8:44). The name *Christian* was a nickname given by unbelievers in Antioch to believers in Christ more out of mockery than respect. This was the first time they were called by this name (Acts 11:26). The Romans in New Testament times spoke Latin, and *ianos* was joined to a slave's name who carried his master's name, thus indicating he would obey his commands. This was also true of a soldier who carried his officer's name to show he would follow his orders. "Christian" meant a "servant of Jesus Christ," or a "soldier under Christ's command."[34] Used three times in Scripture, a Christian is one by—

Choice. One does not become a Christian by physical birth, nor by the will of the flesh (mind) nor by the will of man or a Church creed, but by repentance, believing in and receiving Jesus Christ as their own personal Savior (John 1:12,13; John 3:16).

Change. Christians had various names such as *Believers, Children of God, Disciples, Saints*, etc, but a change came when they were first called "Christians" in Antioch. Upon one's accepting Christ as their Savior, a change took place as they became a new creature (creation) with old things passing away and all things becoming new (II Corinthians 5:17).

Challenge, to be bold under all circumstances (I Peter 4:12–16).

—To bear Christ's reproach (I Timothy 4:10; Hebrews 13:13).
—To press on, growing into maturity (Philippians 3:14; II Peter 3:18).

Christians have been raised to walk in newness of life, which means they are to "Come out from among sinners and be *separate*, so says God. and touch not the unclean thing" (Romans 6:4; II Corinthians 6:17). Sinners, the followers of Satan, are dead in trespasses and in sin. They walk after the things of the world—the lust of the flesh, the lust of the eyes and the pride of life. Admonishing the Christian to obey the "Principle of Separation," he is not to "touch the unclean thing," the things of the world which are common to the sinner. There must be a clean break from their old sinful way as well as a clean break from their unsaved companions. This does not mean to annihilate one's self completely from sinners. We are to hate their sins but love them for Christ's sake, seeking to win them to Him.

In writing to the people of Corinth, they had been saved from immorality and idolatry. Paul sought to let them know there had to be total separation from the old way of life to a new one in Christ. He was pleading for a Christian Church made up of separated believers, not of people who professed Christ with their mouth and still lived their old sinful ways. They had to be separated from this old way to keep them from remaining "babes in Christ," separated from things that would stunt their spiritual growth. "Growth in grace and knowledge of our Lord and Savior Jesus" is a command related to "be separated" (II Peter 3:18). Our obedience to these laws enable us to "mortify our members" (Colossians 3:5). *Mortify* means "put to death" to "die daily to self but alive unto Christ" (I Corinthians 15:31b).

Believers must never forget they still live in their fleshly bodies, hence the possibility of yielding to some "old" habit or way of life before they were saved. The apostle Paul had this problem. In addressing the Romans, he said in effect, "I endorse and delight in God's law in my inner man. But I see a different law in the members of my body." *Members* of our bodies refer to belonging to the earth and are instruments of sin. Continuing, Paul said these members at times wage war against the law of my mind and there are times I desire to do good but do not. The appetites and wills of the sensitive flesh are ever present (Romans 7:22,23). In situations such as these, what was Paul's remedy? Realizing he was a new creature in Christ, a possessor of Christ's mind (I Corinthians 2:16b), he raised the question, "Who will release me from the shackles of this body of death?" The answer:

> "Thank God, He will through Jesus Christ our Lord. So then I of myself with Christ's mind and my heart serve the law of God," or His "Principle of Separation" (Romans 7:24,25). The "Principle of Separation" involves several areas of our relationship with God:

1. Godly Living. Christ is the believer's example in the matter of separation from the world, the flesh and the devil as we follow in His footsteps (I Peter 2:21). Scripture outlines numerous things a believer should do to show he means business for the Lord, things which prove that he is wholly dedicated unto Him. A Christian must—[35]

—Claim his redemptive rights by being a servant of righteousness: Romans 6:11–18.

—Lay hold of the full equipment for satanic warfare by putting on the whole armor of God: Ephesians 6:11–18. God's whole armor protects only the front of the believer; the back is exposed. The Christian is always to advance, *never* retreat. If we turn and flee we have no protection. We must:

—Maintain self-control, mastering our enemy: Ephesians 4:27.
—Abide under the shadow of the Almighty: Psalm 91:1–3.

The Principle of Separation

- —Watch and pray that we enter not into temptation: Matthew 26:41.
- —Continually exercise faith in Christ: Romans 1:17; I John 5:1–5.
- —Claim God's promises: Philippians 4:13,19.
- —Be vigilant (watchful, alert): I Peter 5:8
- —Resist Satan and his tactics: James 4:7.
- —Put on the Lord Jesus Christ and make no provisions for the flesh. This will enable us to have decisive victories, gain new territory, possess the spoils of victory and live on "resurrection territory" and have positive and ever greater conquests.
- —To honor and respect the "Captain" of our lives, Jesus Christ. God may allow Satan to act as a drill sergeant with his army, but the *Captain* of His good soldiers ranks above the sergeant (II Timothy 2:3).
- —Exercise faith for victory on earth with the promise of final triumph and eternal reward.

Having been raised to walk in newness of life (Romans 6:4), we are to seek those things which are above where Christ sits on the right hand of God. Our affection must be set on things above, not on things below—on worldly things. Positionally, we are dead to self and our life is hid with Christ in God (Colossians 3:1–3). We put our position into practice when we separate ourselves from things below by dying to—[36]

- —Self, being crucified with Christ: Romans 6:6; Galatians 2:20.
- —Sin: Romans 6:11a.
- —The flesh: Galatians 5:24.
- —The devil and principalities and powers. When the seventy disciples returned from their mission, Jesus said He had given them *power* over all the *power* of the enemy (Luke 9: 1;10:19). *Power of the enemy* is *dunamis* in Greek, from which we get the word dynamite. Yes, Satan's power is very powerful but the *power* Christ gave His disciples is *exousia*, which means authority. Christ's authoritative power, which is our power, far exceeds Satan's. We must note that, although Satan has been defeated, the things mentioned above which he uses against us are not dead—self, sin and the flesh. It is the believer who is dead to these things, having been made alive with God through Christ by being—
- —Buried with Christ: Romans 6:4a,5.
- —Resurrected—risen with Christ: Colossians 3:1; Romans 6:4b.

By our being "dead" to the above, we are putting off the "old man" and putting on the "new man" (Colossians 3:5–23).
The "old man" puts off—

- —Evil passions of the flesh: vss. 5–7.
- —Evil actions of the mind: vss. 8, 9.

The "new Man" puts on—

- —Desires to be a fruit-bearer: vs. 12.
- —Consideration of others: vss. 13,14.
- —Faithfulness with the family in the home: vss. 18–21.
- —Obedience to his Lord and Master: vss. 22,23.

Having considered Biblical statements regarding Christian living as a separated believer, the following reveals how best one may live a separated life. To ignore what God outlines for His children to prove what they say they believe is to play into Satan's hands. To follow this list will cause those who are still in darkness to see the light of salvation in our lives, taking note of the fact that we have been with Jesus: Acts 4:13.

1. *Fear* the Lord and serve Him in sincerity and in truth: Joshua 24:14. "Fear" means to show reverence for and worshiping only the Lord; also to—

- —Choose the Lord over all: Joshua 24:15.
- —Make vows unto the Lord and *keep* them: Joshua 24:24; Ecclesiastes 5:4,5.

2. Walk as children of light: Ephesians 5:8–14.

- —Manifesting the fruit of the Spirit: vss. 8–10.
- —Having no fellowship with the unfruitful works of darkness, but rather rebuke them: vss. 11,12.
- —Circumspectly—carefully, accurately, turning neither to the left nor to the right: Ephesians 5:15a; Joshua 1:7,8.—not as fools: vs. 15b.
- —Not as Gentiles: Ephesians 4:17.
- —Not after the flesh: Romans 8:1b.
- —Not by sight: II Corinthians 5:7.
- —Not in rioting (misbehavior; to walk honestly): Romans 13:13.
- —Not in craftiness (scam; trickery): II Corinthians 4:2.

But by using wisdom, redeeming the time in doing the will of God: Ephesians 5:16–18.

- —Worthy of our vocation—our heavenly calling: Ephesians 4:1. Listed are various qualifying traits of this calling in Philippians 4:2–8—
- —Rejoice always: vs. 4.
- —Be considerate of others: vss. 5a; 2:3,4e
- —Be careful (anxious) for nothing: vs. 6a.
- —Pray about everything: vs. 6b.
- —Be thankful for everything, regardless: vs. 6c.
- —Enjoy God's peace: vs. 7.
- —Be truthful and honest: vs. 8a.

The Principle of Separation 91

—Be just: 8b.
—Be pure: vs. 8c.
—Be lovely: vs. 8d.
—Have a good report: vs. 8e.
—Have a deep spiritual life: vs. 8f.
—Always praise God from whom all blessings flow: vs. 8g.
—Be ready for Christ's coming: vs. 8b with I John 2:28.
—Think (meditate) *on* these things and *do* them: vs. 8h. Is it possible to do all this? See Philippians 4:13 and Mark 9:23.

2. Separation from Unbelievers (II Corinthians 6:14). For a Christian to be linked with unbelievers means putting one in a compromising position. Righteousness can have no partnership with unrighteousness. There can be no fellowship of light with darkness, no harmony with Satan and his demons, nothing in common with idolaters. Compromise involves watering down the Gospel—either adding to it or subtracting from it. Woe be to anyone who preaches any other gospel than the pure Gospel of Christ (Galatians 1:9). Those who are in the "Modernist's School" are guilty of this as they either change the Word of God to suit their fancy or deny portions of Scripture completely. The tragedy is that many people are led astray and are looking for a pastor who is a "good mixer," someone who is versatile, adept, can lead singing, direct the choir, work with the young people, be a good counselor, make visits, who can adapt to any situation, attend all social events, be a good executive and preach sermonettes on current events. God, however, is looking for a man who adheres to sound Biblical doctrine in feeding his flock, one who studies and prays, who sets a good example—not in being a "good mixer" but by being a "good separator" by practicing what he preaches (II Corinthians 6:14-18).

The Scripture gives some "down home" illustrations about "compromise," things that are "unequally yoked or joined together." Note Leviticus 19:19b.[37]

1. Do not mix full-bred cattle with any half-breeds (19a). This tends to breed an inferior stock. When believers tend to mix with lukewarm, cold, unbelieving people, apathy and apostasy soon follow. Many Israelites fell in the wilderness because of a *mixed multitude* (Exodus 12:38; Numbers 11:4a).

2. Do not mix seed in planting (19b). This tends to take away the true value and taste of the grain or fruit and results in a weakness of strength by those whose life is dependent upon it. The Word of God, which is the Seed for the promotion of life and growth, cannot be mixed with human wisdom (Luke 8:11; I Corinthians 2:4,5). Only as the pure Seed of God's Word is planted and men "taste and see that the Lord is good" can there be an excellent reaping of a fruit harvest in the lives of believers (Psalm 34:8; John 15:7,8).

3. Do not mix material in clothing (19:19c). Mixed fabrics soon fill with creases and folds due to uneven shrinkage and the garment wears out in uneven places. We are not to mix the fine linen of Christ's righteousness with the wool of the world. We are not to love the things of the world, the lust of the flesh, the lust of eye and the pride of life (I John 2:15-17).

3. Unity in Marriage. Believers are not to marry unbelievers which puts them in a position of being "unequally yoked together." Marriage is a true picture of Christ and His believing Bride (Ephesians 5:21–33). The children of Israel were forbidden to marry strangers—those who were not Israelites (Deuteronomy 25:5; Nehemiah 13:12). Intermarriage with unbelievers or those of a cult or another religion will present grave problems not only between husband and wife but in rearing their children in a "divided" home. It is said that "love in blind but marriage is the eye opener." Too often divorce follows such situations. It is a sin for a true believer to be joined with a non-believer for to do so breaks the "Principle of Separation—be not unequally yoked together with unbelievers" (II Corinthians 6:14).

4. Worshiping Idols. Separation involves "keeping ourselves from idols" (I John 5:21). John here is speaking to Christians, not heathens. This is a warning he gives after outlining numerous rules for godly living and loving one another, as noted in his Epistle. Idolators—[38]

> Forget God: Deuteronomy 8:19.
> Are vain in their imaginations: Romans 1:21–23.
> Are carried away with their dumb idols: I Corinthians 12:2.
> Pollute the name of God: Ezekiel 20:13.
> Are estranged from God: Ezekiel 14:5.
> Hate God: II Chronicles 19:2.
> Have fellowship with devils (demons): I Corinthians 10:20.
> Break the first and second commandments: Exodus 20:2,3.

After considering what idolators do in worship, it might seem strange that John told Christians to "keep yourselves from idols." However, religions have idols their subjects pray to, bow down to and pay them homage. Candles are lit as prayers are made before statues, prayers repeated over and over for deceased "saints" to pray for them. Paul as Saul of Tarsus worshiped his Jewish religion, which became an idol to him (Philippians 3:4–6). We don't know exactly what idols John had in mind when he warned Christians about them, but there are idols of-

> —Images: Acts 17:29.
> —Self: Mark 8:34–38.
> —Family members: Luke 14:26.
> —Man: Galatians 1:10.
> —Money: Matthew 6:24; I Timothy 6:10.
> —Worldliness (lust, pride, sports, gambling, etc): I John 2:15–17. God's remedy for keeping one's self from idols are:
> —Trust Him as His remnant did in not worshiping the god Baal of the ancient Canaanites: I Kings 19:18 with Romans 11:4.
> —Obey God's commandments, not just those that suit us, but *all:* Exodus 20:1–17.

The Principle of Separation 93

- —Keep self from any and all idols: I John 5:21; 2:17.
- —Flee all kinds: I Corinthians 10:14.
- —Testify boldly against as Paul and Barnabas did when Paul healed a lame man and the people wanted to make him and Barnabas idols and worship them: Acts 14:8–18.

5. Local Church Separation. Nothing is wrong with a Church taking a fundamental, separate stand when it comes to sound Biblical doctrine, proper Church discipline and its stand against immorality and the breaking of God's laws. Its purpose of being founded is to propagate the Gospel of the Lord Jesus Christ to win the lost to Him and edify the saints. We find this to be the pattern of the New Testament Churches.

If the question is raised that a separated Church and its Biblical stand is narrow-minded, we need to consider the writers of the Bible. Israel had gotten into such a spiritual slump with unorthodox priests that God had to raise up prophets to get these people to see the light. The writers of the Epistles often had to "tell it like it is," to get some believers to walk in a manner pleasing to the Lord. Christ was so narrow minded He said "I am *the* Way, *the* Truth and *the* Life, no man can come unto the Father *but by* Me" (John 14:6). His Gospel is the *only* means of one being saved from a devil's hell. There are no "ifs, ands or buts" in God's one way of salvation. Narrow-minded, yes but it is the truth. Paul's narrow-mindedness verified the statements of Christ when he told those at Ephesus that it is *only* by grace through faith that one is saved and that not of himself, not of his own works lest he should boast (2:8,9). He said a person could not have peace with God unless he was justified by faith (Romans 5:1). Peter said no one could be saved except through the name of Jesus (Acts 4:12). The writer of Hebrews also verifies Christ is the only Savior (1:3).

God's Word, the Bible, presents the only truth for man to follow to become a Christian and live in a Christian manner. Jesus said the world hated Him, and would hate us (John 15:18). This is due to our separation, our narrow-mindedness in standing for the truth. Unless we follow God's instructions in obeying the "Principle of Separation," the world has every right to say to us what Jesus said to the hypocritical Pharisees, "You draw near unto Me with your mouth and you honor Me with your lying lips, but your heart is far from Me. But in vain do you worship Me, teaching the doctrine of the commandments of men" [not the commandments of Scripture]" (Matthew 15:7–9).

Unless a Church has separated members and has established itself as a Bible believing, Bible preaching Church, fundamental and separated from other Churches that follow manuals, creeds and statements of faith that water down the Scriptures to appease people, it might as well close its doors. But thank God for pastors and members whose desire it is to serve God and Him only and seek to make Him and His Son known to others.

6. Needed, a Revival. There seems to be two groups of believers today. One group seeks to follow the pattern of those in New Testament times while the other group seems to go to an extreme of isolating those who do not believe what their rules specify. As a result of this division, there is not the unity of the faith and no spirit of revival in our land among those who hold to the basic teachings of Scripture.

There is always the possibility a Church can take a law in their own hands and carry it too far, thus becoming too ultra-legalistic. The Pharisees would often interpret God's laws to suit the natural mind and would fall into Satan's trap of ignoring the simple law they should follow. Some today have laws for members that go beyond the very purpose of the establishment of a Church—far beyond the laws of God.

John gives us an example of a Church that appeared to have a good testimony for their faith and works—their service to the Lord. They were able to test those who said they were of the faith. They had become content to be "pew warmers" in attendance, letting one truth go in one ear and out the other. The local Church at Ephesus had lost the one thing needed to make them effective in their outreach as a Gospel Church. They had lost or "left their first love" (Revelation 2: 1-4). They did not retain that strong affectionate love for God and sacred things which they first had when they came to a knowledge of the truth of being justified by faith in Christ. They also left their first love for the lost and their evangelistic fire vanished.

There are ultra-fundamental Churches scattered throughout America. While holding to the cardinal truths of the Christian faith, much has been added that sets them apart from other sound Churches. I know of a Church in Maryland that posts a "sentry" on the Church steps to keep ladies who wear slacks from entering the service. In the south some ultra-Baptist Churches allow only a descendant of John the Baptist to baptize converts. Some say only the King James Version Bible can be used since it is the only Bible "God would read." Some narrow-minded ones do not permit women to speak one word once they enter the Church, this in view of women remaining silent in discussing doctrinal matters. Men's hair can be just a certain length and any form of make-up on a woman is forbidden. The tragedy of some of these laws is that people are driven away, vowing they will not go to any Church if that is what Christianity is all about. Suffice it to say, Churches like this have "left their first love."

The Remedy for Revival

After John told those at Ephesus of their true spiritual state, he followed in verse five saying : "*Remember*. go back in your thinking to the time you were first saved. Consider the state of grace in which you once stood. Think of the happiness, love, joy which you once experienced when you received remission of your sins and the zeal you had for God's glory and the salvation for lost mankind. Remember too, your willing, obedient spirit, your cheerful self-denial, your fervor in private prayer, your detachment from the world and your heavenly-mindedness. *Remember* and consider all these things."[39]

After telling them to remember all the delights of their conversion, he then admonishes them to "Remember the loss you have sustained in falling from such blessings and repent, being deeply humbled before God for being so self-centered and not guarding your Divine treasury. When you repent, remember your first work—resume your former zeal and diligence, watch, pray, reprove sin, carefully attend to all the ordinances of God, walk as in His sight, and rest not till you have recovered all your lost ground and have gotten back the evidence of your acceptance of Christ."

While it is true that Christ said the "gates of hell would not prevail against the Church" (Matthew 16:18a), the thought here is that the powers of Satan would not overcome the Church. Yet when a Church is weakened due to extremism and isolation such as the illustrations given, there is a need for a Spirit-filled revival among the saints. Better to be separate as per the instructions of God's Word than to be guilty of losing first love.

How badly does America need a revival? Why is there such a great need for believers in America to be separated unto God and on the alert as they live daily for the Lord? We are told that "righteousness exalts a nation but sin is a reproach to any people" (Proverbs 14:34). Our history shows that our founding fathers followed closely Biblical principles in organizing this nation. However, over a period of time due to free thought, evolution, and lowering of morals, our land is in bad shape today. Christians have been given a back seat and just about anything goes today, not only in homes, in schools, in business but in our own Government as well. The general opinion is "So what, who cares." Morals are at an all-time low and the majority of people seem to care nothing about sex-permissivism, pre-sex marriage, same sex marriage (even by some pastors), homosexuality, lesbianism, abortion (child sacrifice), perjury, drinking, illegal drugs, etc.

Our Constitution says "Congress shall make no law respecting the establishment of religion or prohibiting the free exercise thereof or abridging the freedom of free speech." To interpret this to mean "Separation of Church and State" as our Supreme Court and the ACLU have done is idiotic. Prayer in school is prohibited even when a child says the blessing before eating. In no way is the child seeking to establish a Church on government property. The same is true if a student carries a Bible to school with his text books. Chief Justice William Rehnquist stated "the phrase, 'separation of church and state,' is a misleading metaphor which should be frankly and explicitly abandoned." He labels it "a mischievous diversion of judges from the actual intentions by the drafters of the Bill of Rights." I wonder why the Chief Justice hasn't brought about a vote to repeal the Court's decision of "Separation of State and Church?" When a teacher is not permitted to have a Bible on his/her desk and kids can't discuss the meaning of Christmas, or a City cannot celebrate a "Bible Week," something is wrong with the laws our government makes.

Wake up America! Better yet, wake up Churches, separate yourselves unto God's laws. Become "fools for Christ's sake" if necessary to prove that Christianity is real, vital, and essential for America to get back to God and live according to His Word and not man-made laws. *My oh my, what a need to pray for a revival!* Yieldedness on our part will help to bring it about. It starts coming down *vertically* from heaven into our hearts but it has to be worked out *horizontally* to be effective where needed. It has happened before and it can happen again through me—through *you*.

7. Resisting Satan. The arch enemy of all fundamental Churches is Satan himself. His desire is to defeat every child of God. If he could, and did, sway Peter to deny the Lord three times after his confession that Jesus was the Son of God, there is no reason why Satan or his demons could not influence other children of God. If the child of God is not subject to his influence,[40] why-

> —Put on the whole armor of God? Ephesians 6:11.
> —Wrestle against wicked spirits? Ephesians 6:12.
> —Take the shield of faith to ward off his fiery darts? Ephesians 6:16.
> —Give no place to the devil? Ephesians 4:27
> —Be sober and vigilant? I Peter 5:8.
> —Not to be lifted up with pride? I Timothy 3:6.
> —Submit yourselves to God and resist Satan? James 4:7.
> —Have a good report? I Timothy 3:7

Satan is so deceptive ho can transform himself into an angel of light, his ministers (demons) can be changed into ministers of righteousness, and he can transform false prophets and deceitful workers into the apostles of Christ (II Corinthians 11:13–15). Believers are to take the attitude of confidence toward their adversary, the devil, relying upon God's provision and power through Christ for victory over him. A believer, filled with God's Spirit, living a victorious life over the world, the flesh and the devil, needs only to rebuke Satan and his emissaries "in the name of Jesus and the power of His blood." When Peter and John healed a lame man (Acts 3:1–8), they were asked this question by the Pharisees, "By what *power* or what *name* have you done this?" Peter answered, "By the name of Jesus Christ of Nazareth, Whom you crucified." (Acts 4:7–11). Christ's crucifixion speaks of the *power* of His blood, giving us the example needed to resist Satan in Christ's name and the power of His blood. Thank God a *separated* believer can resist Satan, refute his demons with God's Word like Christ did in the wilderness (Matthew 4:1–11). By so appropriating God's power we become "more than conquerors through Christ who loves us" (Romans 8:37). What a sight to see Satan fleeing from us when we resist him!

CONCLUSION

Whenever a study is made on a certain subject in school, a test is given to find out what the student learned. Since we are in the "School of God," we have studied in this chapter the "Principle of Separation." It is appropriate that we give ourselves—

A Test for Glorifying God

We read in Colossians "And whatsoever you do in word and deed, do all to the glory of God in the name of the Lord Jesus, giving thanks through Him to God the

The Principle of Separation 97

Father" (3:17). The following questions demand honest answers and only one who is obeying the "Principle of Separation" will pass.

> —Will what I am about to do or say or where I am about to go enslave me for wrong?
> —Will such strengthen my faith in Christ and the Word of God?
> —Will it cause others to get a foggy view of Christ?
> —Can I really do it for the glory of God?
> —Can I witness to others of Christ while participating?
> —Will these things keep me away from duty in my own Church?

Separated Christians are the only Christ sinners see, they are the only Bible they will ever read until they become born again. We are Living Epistles, read and known of all men (II Corinthians 3:2,3)[41]

—As a letter is written on prepared material, so the Christian is God's prepared material upon which He writes His message of being conformed to the image of His dear Son: Romans 8:29.

—As a letter must be free of blots so the reader can get the full import of the message, so the Christian must be unspotted by the flesh if the message of salvation is to be understood: Jude 23b.

—As the writer of the letter is recognized by the style of handwriting, so the sinner recognizes a Christian by his style of godly living: Titus 2:12.

—As a letter bears the expression of the writer, so the Christian must bear about in his body the life of Christ: II Corinthians 4:10–13.

—As a letter bears the signature of the writer, so the Christian puts his name on the line for God—"Yet not I, but Christ in me:" I Corinthians 15:10; Galatians 2:20.

—As a letter bears the time of writing (date), so the Christian in season and out of season sends forth the message of *salvation—now is the day*: II Timothy 4:2; II Corinthians 6:2.

—As a letter bears an address, so the Christian reveals a message of direction—the straight and narrow road that leads to eternal life: Matthew 7:14; Proverbs 3:6.

—As a letter is sealed and bears a proper stamp to assure readiness for delivery, so the Christian, as debtor to all men, is stamped with the responsibility of readiness to preach the Gospel to every creature: Romans 1:14–16 with Matthew 28:19,20.

> "You are writing a Gospel
> A chapter each day,
> In deeds that you do
> And words that you say.
> Men read what you write
> Whether false or true;

Say—What is the Gospel
According to you?[42]

The late Dr. Wilbur Chapman said: "The thing that governs my life is this: Anything that dims my vision of Christ, or takes away my taste for Bible study, or cramps my prayer life, or makes Christian work difficult, *is wrong for me*, and I must, as a Christian turn away from it. This simple rule may help you find a safe path for you along life's highway."

A Prayer Thought

We can prove we are obeying the *Principle of Separation* by not going anywhere we wouldn't want to be found when Christ returns, not doing anything we wouldn't want to be doing when He comes, and not saying anything we wouldn't want to be saying when He descends from heaven at the Rapture for His own.

> Dear Lord, help me to be so obedient to Your Principle of Separation that I will have a sweet disposition to show a world blinded by unbelief that my Savior is not a myth but a Savior living in my heart and life. May none ever look at me and say that Christ died in vain. In His precious name I pray. Amen.
> (Colossians 3:1–4)

Chapter Eleven

THE PRINCIPLE OF SOULWINNING

Among the mighty miracles God has performed down through the centuries is that of placing the Church in the world. It is the one institution through which the Holy Spirit can reach the unsaved, and this is done by empowering the children of God to be witnesses of Christ (Acts 1:8). Since the Church began centuries ago, in spite of the hatred and persecution of countless numbers of true believers, you and I have become recipients of the Gospel . All believers, especially those here in America, cannot thank God enough that we have an open Bible and the privilege of religious freedom. We are debtors to the faith of saints of days gone by.

We are debtors to each succeeding generation because they obeyed the "Principle of Soulwinning." They followed Christ's admonition, "Follow Me and I will make you fishers of men" (Matthew 4:19). They were bound by His charge, "Confess me before men and I will confess you before My Father who is in heaven. Deny Me before men and I will deny you before My Father who is in heaven" (Matthew 10:32,33).

When Jesus healed a man who had been possessed with the devil, He told him to "Go home and *tell* others what great things the Lord had done for him" (Mark 5:19). Luke gives the same account, but adds "Go home and *show* them what great things God has done for you" (8:39). This is the foundation for soulwinning—showing others through your life what great things God did for you when you were saved, and *telling* others how God can do great things for them when they accept Christ as their own Savior. We call this Evangelism—"A *show* and *tell* ministry."

The moment one accepts Christ as their Savior his sins are forgiven, his past is blotted out, a new way has been established and a song has been put in his heart. He now has a new song to sing and something to shout about (Psalm 40:2,3; 5:11).

A new born baby knows how to get attention by doing the only thing it knows to do—crying. Mother is attracted to come to assist. As new born babes in Christ, we must begin to "noise" abroad our new song, our *telling* forth of what great things God has done for us. Too often many Christians take a back seat and remain "mum" with the thought "I don't have any training. I haven't had any courses in soulwinning, etc." The idea is to follow Christ and give a simple testimony of your experience in accepting Him. You can tell of your condition being a lost sinner, that Christ died for your sins, but upon confessing your sins to Him and accepting Him as your Savior, you were saved. It is that simple. If you witness an automobile accident and were called to testify in Court, you wouldn't refuse by saying you haven't had a course in "Car Accident Witnessing." You are simply expected to tell only what you saw. In our witnessing for Christ, we start by telling of our experience in coming to Christ to be saved.

Soon you will learn there are certain techniques in the matter of witnessing. No two people are alike. When a fisherman goes fishing he carries certain bait and lures for different kinds of fish. Jude informs us in his Epistle as we contend for the faith, we have to make a difference. On some we have compassion, others we seek to create fear in the individual, but in and under all circumstances, we must be kind and exhibit the love of God (verses 22,23).

When a believer is saved, it is expected that he or she seeks out other believers and becomes united in a Gospel preaching Church. In such a Church, the pastor has a two-fold ministry:

> (1) to expound the Word of God to edify believers and
> (2) be evangelical in his appeal for any present who are not saved to believe on the Lord Jesus Christ. The Apostle Paul gives us this two-fold ministry of edification (Ephesians 4:11–16) and in preaching the Word, doing the work of an Evangelist in seeking the lost (II Timothy 4:2,5).

As a pastor assumes his full responsibility of his ministry, he challenges his flock to be faithful witnesses by visitation, phone calls, letter writing, etc. A believer is to take advantage of every situation, and often times make situations to witness. One thing a faithful pastor will do is to start a—

Discipling Program

Being taught that all believers are saved to serve, in a discipling program members are encouraged to attend this "School of Obedience" to learn better methods of soulwinning. They will be given such promises as: "He that winneth souls is wise" and "they that be wise shall shine as the brightness of the firmament, and they that turn many to righteousness shall shine as the stars for ever" (Proverbs 11:30; Daniel 12:3). God is so appreciative of our winning souls to Christ He will honor us in glory.

Cult members are engaged in spreading their religion, even going from door to door to spread their heresy. We who know Christ have the *truth* and only as we "follow Christ in fishing for men" will others know truth. We are "watchmen" to give a warning to the unsaved of their condition before God and their need of Him. If we don't their blood will be required of us (Ezekiel 3:18,19). If we have no vision people perish (Proverbs 29:18). All God requires of His child is to tell what he knows.

The Principle of Soulwinning

Ambassadors for Christ

A discipling, soul-winning program impresses believers that each is an *Ambassador for Christ* (II Corinthians 5:20). With our citizenship being in heaven, we, as pilgrims and strangers on earth, represent our blessed Savior in a country of sin. As an Ambassador from our country goes to a foreign country to represent America, so God leaves us here on earth for a time to represent Him.

In the training of members to do personal witnessing, there is a need to have experienced soul-winners to be in charge to help train others in the techniques of this ministry. Enthusiasm is a quality that must be handled in such a way that skillful tact must reign instead of attack. Winsomeness must be a key factor or else the "fish" will not come near the bate. It is a tremendous privilege a child of God has to pour out his life into other people and see them as they acknowledge their need of Christ.

As the Discipling Program progresses, believers are challenged to "go thou and do likewise." Dedication is encouraged. All personal desires must be put on the shelf. Christ must be put first to get all the "know-how." Time must be taken at home for study, preparatory to "exam" time." All these efforts are worth it simply because it is all being done as unto the Lord and for His glory.

We repeat again, no two sinners are alike. Various Scripture verses should be memorized to adequately present the simple *plan of salvation*. For example—

> —The "A," "B," C's" of Salvation. "A" is "All have sinned and come short of the glory of God" (Romans 3:23). "B" is *"Believe* on the Lord Jesus Christ and thou shall be saved" (Acts 16:31; John 1:12). "C" is *"Come* unto Me all you who labor and are heavy ladened, and I will give you rest"* (Matthew 11:28)
>
> —"The Roman Road." "There is none righteous, no not one" (Romans 3:10–18). "The wages of sin is death" (Romans 6:23a). "Call upon the Lord to be saved" (Romans 10:13). "The gift of God is eternal life" (Romans 6:23b).
>
> —"Four Principles of Salvation." *Principle One.* God loves every human being and has given in His Word a wonderful plan for their lives (John 3:16; Romans 5:6–8). *Principle Two.* Man is sinful and separated from God. He needs to know *why* God loves him (Romans 3:23; John 3:36; Romans 6:23b). *Principle Three.* Christ is God's *only* provision for sinful man; He is the *only* Way (John 14:6; Acts 4:12).*Principle Four.* Man must, by choice, believe in and receive Jesus Christ as his Lord and Savior (John 1:12; Romans 10:9,10). Scripture has many verses to help an unsaved person see what his spiritual need is. The Holy Spirit is ever present to help make known God's Word and convict of sin as we note in Proverbs 1:23–33 and John 16:7–9.

Once the individual is saved there must be instructions to help this one. Memorized Scripture helps, but a Bible (or at least a New Testament) should always be in readiness to let the person "read" for himself/herself what is needed to be seen. Verses must be shown what the *newness of life* is that must be lived to establish that their decision was real. They can be shown how to grow in the things of the Lord. They cannot be "fed" too much at the outset, but "follow-ups" from time to time help. It is not wise to tell them they are saved upon acceptance of Christ, but by all means use Scripture to show them what God says. This information should be received from God, not you. Use such verses as John 1:12; 5:24. Notice the present tense of the words *hath* and *is passed* in 5:24. Both I John 5:12.13 and II Timothy 1:12 give assurance that we can *know* we are saved, having placed our trust in Christ. These verses give God's assurance that if their decision was valid, *they are uaved*. If they can pinpoint the place and time of their decision, they can always rebuff Satan when he tries to tell them how foolish they are for thinking they are saved. Regardless of one's remembering a time and place there is always God's Word to give us the assurance needed.

Scripture Memorization

In studying our Bible to be qualified to reach others with God's truth, it is essential to memorize certain verses in dealing with the lost. Not only will these verses help the believer to see that they were saved to serve, it enables him to show himself approved unto God, a workman who needs not to be ashamed (II Timothy 2:15). Paul tells us that those who believe on Christ shall not be ashamed (Romans 10:11 with 1:16). In knowing the Word and by rightly dividing it, Paul keeps presenting himself to the Lord as a living sacrifice and allows such following verses to govern his life:

- —Doing all things through Christ who strengthens him: Philippians 4:13.
- —Always ready to "say so" about his redemption: Psalm 107:2.
- —Always make sure when telling others about Christ they can tell you are living for and walking with Him: I Corinthians 6:19,20; I Peter 1:21.
- —Praying daily to have a compassion for the lost. Compassion was one thing that motivated Christ to reach people in need (Matthew 9:36).
- —Keeping in mind that the fields are white unto harvest but the laborers are few (John 4:35 with Matthew 9:37).
- —The Lord has a job for each of His children, but never let the following be said of you.

HE'S LOST[43]

Around the corner I have a friend
In this great city that has no end,
And he's lost—a fine young man,
But he's lost! And I always plan

> To speak to him about God's love,
> Of Christ who came down from above,
> And how He died on the Cross to pay
> The sinner's debt. I think daily,
> Somehow I must speak my heart to Jim;
> Tomorrow I'll have a talk with him.
> My friend is lost; he does not know
> The peril he risks; he must not go
>
> Year after year like this and die
> Before I tell him how truly I
> Desire to see him give God his heart,
> To repent, believe, get a new start.
> But tomorrow comes and tomorrow goes
> Distance between us grows and grows.
> Around the corner—yet miles away. . . .
> "Here's a telegram, Sir. . . ."
> "Jim died yesterday."
> While I delayed, thus came the end:
> Jim lost his soul; Christ lost a friend!

The Apostle Paul set a good example for us in the matter of soulwinning. He made certain he met with people and got the message across. Some believed on Christ, some rejected Him, but he "pressed on," he "persuaded" his hearers (Philippians 3:14; II Corinthians 5:ha). He fought a good fight and he stayed on course (II Timothy 4:7). We cannot make people believe, but in sowing the *Seed* of God's Word in their hearts we can let them know that God loves then, *that He wants them*. This is when we have to turn them completely over to the Holy Spirit for God to keep working with them.

Giving Out Tracts

A very useful tool in witnessing is giving a tract to those with whom you are witnessing. It should be one with a short story about someone who had an experience with Christ and giving the plan of salvation. Most folks like something short and to the point. But regardless, the Holy Spirit can lead you to have several, one of which will suit the occasion. I would like to give a few examples how tracts played an important roll in leading some to Christ.

One never knows why God works in mysterious ways His wonders to perform. He knows exactly how to engineer circumstances for our good and His glory. I was born and raised in a Christian home. Going through Sunday School we had to memorize verses and chapters of Scripture. When I got old enough to "do my thing" as a teen-ager, I quit going to Church and began to live a worldly life. In my early twenties, as a traveling salesman, I arrived in Ashville, NC. My path crossed that of a total stranger but we struck up a conversation. After a few questions, he abruptly looked me straight in the eye and said, "I bet you have a Christian mother back home praying for you." I was shocked at his remark but in composing myself I replied "yes." Asked why I hadn't answered her prayers, I said I have some things in my life to straighten out first and then I'll get right with the Lord. Asked if I were sick would I get well first and then go to a Doctor, I could only say, "no, I'd go when I'm sick." He reminded me I needed to go to Christ with my sins *now*, confess them and let Christ forgive me. At this point he had to leave for work. He thanked me for our conversation and then gave me a list of excuses that people give for not accepting Christ as their Savior, saying "I'll be praying for you."

I was glad to see him go, but as I looked over the Scripture verses that refuted the excuses, I couldn't handle them. Under such conviction, at 3:00 p.m., February 17, 1938, I bowed my heart, confessed I was the sinner for whom Christ died, and trusted Him as my Savior. The next morning I drove to my home in Charlotte to tell my mother I had answered her prayers—I was saved. When I knocked on the door and she saw me standing there, she asked what I was doing home. I told her I had something to tell her, to which she said, "I know." I said "you know what?" When she said "you are saved," I asked "How do you know?" She said yesterday afternoon I got down on my knees and told the Lord I wasn't getting up till He gave me assurance my boy was going to be saved. Soon my heart was flooded with joy that my prayer was answered. I asked what time this happened. She said when I got up, wiped my tears, I heard the clock on the mantle striking 3:00 p.m. What a reunion time my mother and I had when we embraced each other. I had become a trophy of God's grace in answer to my mother's prayers. The Lord used the Seed she had sown, the soulwinner in Ashville watered that Seed, but God, thank Him, gave the increase! I don't remember who this fellow was, but thankfully, one day I'll meet him in glory.

One thing I learned from this experience was this: always carry tracts with me no matter where I go. There are opportunities at filling stations, in super markets, in restaurants, garages—no matter where one goes. In my traveling ministry, one day I got on the Pennsylvania Turnpike at Reading, PA. When the man at the toll booth gave me a ticket, I asked what the ticket was for (of course I knew). He said it shows how much you owe when you get off. I said I thought things were free in America and he said, "Not on this Turnpike!" I gave him a ticket that said, "This is a free ticket. It's not good for anything, it's just free." He laughed and asked what the meaning of the rest of the tract said—"But God's gift is free, it is eternal life through Christ." By this time a car behind me tooted but the toll man stuck his hand out the window and waved at the folks to wait. I took about a minute to give him the plan of salvation and said I'd be praying for him. As I pulled out I stopped on the side of the road while my wife prayed and asked the Lord to water the Seed and bring him to Christ.

Three months later when I was in a meeting in Reading, a man came up to me after the service and asked if we had met before. Recognizing my Southern drawl, he asked if I had ever been on the Pennsylvania Turnpike and given a *Free Ticket* the toll man? I said "yes" and he said, "Well, I'm that man. When I went

The Principle of Soulwinning

home and told my wife, she excitedly said, 'my prayers have been answered. I knew someday someone would get to you with the Gospel!' Two weeks later I accepted Christ as my Savior. We now have a family altar and I'm learning how to witness to others, hoping that I will be able to do for them what you did for me."

I praise the Lord for all that has been accomplished with the usage of tracts. While my wife and I were traveling to a meeting we stopped at a restaurant in Winchester, VA. Noticing the name of the waitress on a pin, I addressed her by name with a smile and asked if she knew who I was. Giving a silly grin, she said "Of course not." I handed her a little card which said. "If you never know me, you'll miss nothing, but if you never know Christ, you'll miss everything—heaven too." She made no expression but stuck the card in her pocket. Before we finished our meal, she came and said she was off duty and asked if she could sit down and ask us a few questions. She said she had heard a sermon sometime ago that bothered her and wondered if we could help her. After she opened up her heart, we had the happy privilege of leading her to the Lord. We had prayer together and gave her some verses to learn and suggested she get in a good Bible preaching Church. What a joy that was to our hearts when she gave her heart to Christ.

One more illustration. While pastoring a Church near Binghamton, NY, we had a weekly T.V. Program. When we concluded one Sunday program, a lady called and asked if we would come and tell her how to apply the message. When we saw her she said she was Catholic and wanted to believe the Gospel as we preached it, but in her troubled mind her priest had told her just to say the Rosary, attend Mass and she would be fine. I told her I couldn't discuss the matter with her unless we used a Catholic Bible. I knew the priest would refute all Scripture I used if I used my Bible. When I showed her verses from her Bible about salvation by grace through faith, she was under such conviction she could almost tell me what the verses said without reading them. Verses I showed her were just like our King James Version. After giving her the simple plan of salvation from the Catholic Bible, she still was hesitant about accepting Christ. In desperation I kept praying silently for her and all of a sudden I remembered in the front of her Bible Pope Leo XIII "Granted to the faithful who spend at least a quarter of an hour in reading the Holy Scriptures with the veneration due to the Divine Word and as spiritual reading, an indulgence of three years.

She said I think an indulgence has to do with time off for good behavior from Purgatory. I asked how old she was and she said she was 18. I told her the average age for a human was 70 years according to Psalm 91:10. I said if you read your Bible for 15 minutes daily for one year, that means you would get 1,095 years off. Multiply that by 52 and the total is 56,940 years. By this time she was beginning to look pale. Reminding her of 13 leap year days, she had to add 39 more years. By this time she screamed "My God, my God, how many more years would I have to spend to get that much time off for good behavior?" Answering that I didn't know, she immediately slipped to her knees, confessed herself as a sinner before God and trusted Christ as her Savior. She turned her back on Catholicism and immediately started living by her own Bible like Martin Luther did!

CONCLUSION

This may sound like an awful thing to say, but I have often wondered how many souls believers would seek to win to the Lord if they were offered $1,000.00 for each they won. Yet, God offers a "Soulwinners Crown" for our following Christ as "fishers of men.!? The Apostle Paul was responsible for many heathens of Thessalonica turning to God from idols and receiving Christ (I Thessalonians 1:6,9). Because he won them to Christ, he said they were "his Crown of Rejoicing," his glory and joy (I Thessalonians 2:19,20).

I feel like there aren't too many *wise* Christians today. Everybody seems so busy with "things." Even sometimes one can become engaged so much in Church work they don't take the time to witness. Yet the Bible reminds us that "He who wins souls is *wise*" (Proverbs 11:30). Not only does Paul say souls we win to Christ are our "Crown of Rejoicing" but Daniel says if we are wise we will shine as the brightness of the firmament, and they that turn many to righteousness [will shine] as the stars forever (12:3).

Dear reader, how burdened are you for those who do not know Christ? Am sure you have some loved ones who are lost. Do they know you care for their souls? God promises rewards to soulwinners, and the question is, when you stand before the Lord, will you be able to point to anyone you led to Christ? It is our duty to be obedient to the "Principle of Soulwinning" and shame on us if we are not. Any Christian can if he will. A chinaman was asked how he witnessed for the Lord. His reply was, "Me gettie on me knees and me talkie, talkie, talkie to the Lord. Then me gettie on me feet and we walkie, walkie, walkie, and those I meet I talkie, talkie, talkie." Years ago in a large city an old scrub woman named Sophie was wonderfully converted to Christ. She became an out-and-out Christian and tireless winner of souls. A friend of Sophie's thought he'd have some fun with her one day. He professed religion but never did practice it. "Say Sophie," he grinned, "I'd better warn you. You're carrying your religion a bit to far." "Maybe so," she replied, "but you aren't carrying yours far enough!" Almost floored for a moment, the practical joker recovered his balance again. "Maybe not, Sophie, but I saw you yesterday in front of cigar store talking your religion to a wooden Indian." "Well, maybe so." replied Sophie, "my eyes aren't what they used to be. But what if I did? Talking to a *wooden Indian* isn't half as bad as being a *wooden Christian* and never talking to anybody about my precious Savior, Jesus Christ!"

What each child of God needs to do is *"wise up*. Personally, I want all the rewards I can get, especially the "Soulwinners Crown." I do not want them for self, but to lay them at the feet of Jesus and say "Thank you Lord for saving my soul." And then I want to hear Him say, "Well done thou good and faithful servant, enter into the joy of the Lord." What a time of rejoicing that will be, not only having eternal fellowship with the One who loved us and gave His life a ransom for us, but eternal fellowship with those we led to Christ, plus the redeemed of all ages!

The Principle of Soulwinning

When it comes to praying in the matter of our witnessing, there are several things to be considered. We must be ready to be on the *go* where the unbelievers are since they do not *come* to us. We must be prepared with the Word of God and some literature to deal with them. *But especially needed is for us to pray and ask the Lord to give us*

A PASSION FOR SOULS[44]

Give me a passion for souls, dear Lord, a passion to save the lost;
O that Thy love were by all adored, and welcomed at any cost.
Jesus, I long, I long to be winning, men who are lost and constantly sinning;
O may this hour be one of beginning the story of pardon to tell. How shall this passion for souls be mine? Lord make Thou the answer clear;
Help me to throw out the old Lifeline to those who are struggling near.

Chapter Twelve

THE PRINCIPLE OF STEWARDSHIP

Scripture informs us that "it is required of a steward that he be found faithful" (I Corinthians 4:2). The word *steward* comes from a Greek word meaning "manager of one's household," implying one who assumes his/her responsibility. It also includes the word "chamberlain," in Romans 16:27 (KJV), which means *treasury* (NKJV). Basically, the word *steward* applies to *all* believers (I Peter 4:10).

Having considered the above, God is telling us that as His stewards, our responsibility is to give back to Him all that is due Him. This involves not only the giving of ourselves but our giving the full amount of what He requests of us. Are we managers of our household as we should and as His *treasurer* are we giving back to Him the portion that is rightfully his?

The very first thing we should give to him is ourselves. Paul commended the redeemed of the Churches in Macedonia because they "first gave of themselves to the Lord" (II Corinthians 8:1,5). This is the believer's first and foremost responsibility and obligation as a steward. Both Jesus and Paul "hit the nail" on the head in statements they made. Jesus said "whosoever shall save his life [live for self] shall lose it, but whosoever shall lose his life [turn it over to Christ] for My sake and the Gospel's, the same shall save it" [as he follows Christ] (Mark 8:34,35). Paul beseeches us to present our bodies as living sacrifices, holy and acceptable unto God, which is our reasonable service. He also reminds us that we are not our own, that we have been bought with a price. Our bodies are the Temple of God and we should glorify Him with our whole being, not being conformed to this world (Romans 12:1,2; I Corinthians 6:19,20).

Stewardship means we are faithfully giving God first place in our lives by

—Putting self on the altar of sacrifice (Romans 12:1).
—Showing forth the praises of Him who called us out of darkness into His marvelous light (I Peter 2:9b).
—Being a student of His Word (II Timothy 2:14).
—Loving God and others (Deuteronomy 6:5).
—Being sanctified (setting self apart unto God: I Thessalonians 4:3a).
—Being forgiving (Ephesians 4:32).

- Being prayer warriors I Thessalonians 5:17).
- Pleasing God as we live by faith (Hebrews 11:6).
- Living a separated life (II Corinthians 6:17).
- Being a soul winner (Matthew 4:19).
- Rejoicing and being thankful (Psalm 97:12; I Thessalonians 5:18).

There is one other requirement we cannot overlook as a steward and it is what is involved in our being God's treasurer—which involves money or finances. In Old Testament times Israel was to give a tithe of her first fruits. This not only involved grain and other commodities to be given unto God for the Levitical priests but also money for the upkeep of the Tabernacle and the Temple. The tithe was one-tenth of whatever was required of them. As we approach the New Testament times we notice what Paul wrote concerning the *collection* in the Churches in Galatia for the poor saints. They were to give on the first day of the week, laying in store as God had prospered them. These people gave liberally (I Corinthians 16:1–3). This leads us to the subject of—

TITHING[45]

Quite a number of scholars in our day teach that tithing is an ordinance under the law and does not apply to us under grace.

- Tithing was *commenced* under Abraham approximately 500 years before the Principle was given when he tithed to Melchizedek (Genesis 14:18–20).
- Tithing was *confirmed* by Moses (Leviticus 18:26).
- Tithing was *commended* by Jesus (Matthew 23:23).
- Tithing is an act of love. It is one way to manifest loyalty to God.
- Tithing is God's carefully made plan for financing His work. That is why He commands it.
- Tithing gives us a part in His program. It is an act of worship.
- Tithing deepens the spiritual life. It gives wisdom in handling His portion of 10%, as well as the remaining portion.
- Tithing teaches us that real giving comes after we give God His 10%, enabling us to trust Him with all that we have.
- Tithing unlocks the windows of heaven for all who will take God at His Word and prove Him (Malachi 3:10).
- Tithing keeps us honest with God so that we do not rob Him (Malachi 3:8).
- Tithing always brings real Christian happiness and blessing when God gets what rightfully belongs to Him.

When Abraham *commenced* giving the tithe to Melchizedek, he honored the Lord with his substance (Proverbs 3:9). When Moses *commanded* the children of Israel to tithe he made it plain they were indebted to God for giving them the vine-

The Principle of Stewardship

yard to honor Him with their increase (Matthew 21:33,34). When Christ *commended* the Pharisees for continuing the tithe, He put His stamp of approval upon this method of giving back to God what was already His (Matthew 23:23). This is what tithing is all about—giving to God what is not mine but "letting go" of what is His. We only give when we give *over and above* the tithe. If the Principle demanded the tithe, how much more blessed is it under grace to give over the tithe.

Where to Give

It is amazing the number of appeals Christians get from various organizations "begging" for donations. True, some are worthy causes, some are done by scam artists. First and foremost, our consideration should be for our local Church of which we are members. If God led us to become a part of a local institution whose leadership is a faithful Bible shepherd, the congregation has a program to support. It needs God's tithe and offerings for support. Each *steward* has a responsibility to assume. If every Church member is obedient to God's "Principle of Giving," their Church will have a sufficient amount for local expenses, plus an abundance for a Missionary Program that supports a number of missionaries in spreading the Gospel. No Radio or Television preacher can do for a local Church what its faithful pastor and members can do under the leadership of the Lord. There are members who don't give to their Church and have bazaars, bake sales, bingo parties, rummage sales to raise finances. They are not "giving." They are "getting for self."

A member who was a chronic complainer said "our Church is costing too much. They're always asking for money. I'm sick and tired of these repeated requests." Another member overhearing him replied: "I want to tell you a story right out of my heart. Some years ago a little boy was born in our home, and from time to time he cost us plenty of money. I had to buy food, medicine, clothes, toys and finally a puppy. When he started to school he cost us plenty more. When he began going with girls and then entered college, you know that took a fortune. In his senior year in college he became quite ill and died. Burial was rather expensive, but from that day 'till this he hasn't cost us a single cent.

"As long as the Church lives and exerts any influence in the world it will cost money. As long as Christianity lives and has influence in your home and community, and remains the 'salt of the earth,' *it will cost money*. Christianity is not costing money in China. They will not allow an open Church there, and when the Church dies for want of support it won't cost you or anyone anything. As long as it lives, it has my support!"

The story is told of a young convert who promised God in the pastor's study that he would give God His tenth the rest of his life, no matter how much he made. As the years rolled by, the one who made this vow unto God became successful and wealthy. He began to become concerned about his vow because he was giving large amounts to his Church each week. He felt he could no longer afford to tithe.

With troubled soul he visited his former pastor, now retired. Explaining the situation to the one who witnessed his vow, he asked the old preacher how he could be released from his vow. It wasn't that he objected giving *some* to the

Church, but he felt he couldn't afford these large amounts. The old preacher slipped to his knees, asking the business man to join him. Looking at him the pastor said, "I don't know how you can be released from your vow, but let us pray that God will reduce your income so you can afford to tithe."

An IRS agent was examining a tax return of a citizen. He was being questioned about the deductions he had made to his Church. In comparison to other details in his return, the $2,600 gift seemed too large. Excusing himself, the agent called the pastor of the Church and asked if "Mr. So and So" gave this amount last year. Looking up the financial record, the pastor soon replied, "He will, he will! What the culprit was doing was going to the Church treasurer each Sunday and getting him to cash a $50.00 check made out to the Church. "Be sure your sin will find you out" (Numbers 32:23).

A Jew and a Gentile had become friends. They decided to take turns going to the Synagogue and the Church. The first Saturday the Gentile went with his Jewish friend to hear the Rabbi. During the service, the Jew put in a ten dollar bill in the offering. The Gentile was observing and put in fifty cents. The next day, which was Sunday, the Jew attended Church with his Gentile friend. When the offering was being taken, the Gentile again put in fifty cents. In a few moments the Jew leaned over and whispered to his Gentile friend, "Almost thou persuadest me to become a Christian!"

> "Once there was a Christian
> He had a pious look;
> His consecration was complete,
> Except his pocket book.
> He'd put a quarter in the plate
> And then with might and maim
> He'd sing, "When we asunder part
> It gives me inward pain."[46]

With all the varied types or methods of giving, there are only three kinds of givers—the flint, the sponge and the honeycomb.

The Flint. To get anything out of a flint you must hammer it, and then you get sparks and chips.

The Sponge. To get anything out of a sponge you must squeeze it. The more you squeeze, the more you get.

The Honeycomb. The honeycomb just overflows with its own sweetness, which is given by a cheerful giver. This is the kind God loves (II Corinthians 9:7).

In our giving to our Church, or "Storehouse" as some call it, it is literally impossible to give support to every Christian work. If stewards are supporting their Church program and it is not in the red, they are obeying the Lord's instructions. It isn't fair for a Church to launch out into a large ministry and beg other churches to support them. We can praise the Lord they have such an ongoing outreach, but it should be limited to their own people. However, if a member has been abundantly blessed by the Lord and feels he has given over and above his responsibility to his own Church, God can give leading and direction to a worthy Christian cause by another group. We should make sure we have confidence in the ministries we are supporting. No matter what we do, we are answerable to God and we want to make sure what we are doing pleases Him.

CONCLUSION

In our consideration of God's "Principle of Stewardship," the two most important things to remember are: "give of ourselves first to the Lord, and then give back to Him what rightfully belongs to Him—His share of the substance." The rich farmer had only one person in mind—himself. He had so much he wanted to build new barns to preserve what he had. He ate, drank and was merry, but when he died overnight, he left it all behind, taking nothing with him (Luke 12:16–21). When we obediently give God what we ought, we are laying up for ourselves treasures in heaven (Matthew 6:19,20). This makes our giving worthwhile.

> What I earned I spent,
> What I saved I lost,
> What I gave I have.

It is so easy to lose interest in a Church in which you have no investment. Unless we back up our service in giving we will label ourselves as stingy Christians and what little we give will be done grudgingly. Someone said, "Does your pocketbook say 'AMEN' when you pray for the Lord's work and you answer your prayer by giving what God has required, *His* tithe and your offering?" in Proverbs 3:9, the writer says-

Honor the Lord with Your Substance[47]

What we have received from the Lord should be dedicated unto Him. Upon everything He has sent our way, may we write, *This is from God*, He gave it to us, He intended it for our good to bless us, to make us happy, to make us Christlike, and we should be grateful and acknowledge Him as our Donor. Every mercy comes from our Father in heaven, and it should lead us to walk worthy of our calling in Christ Jesus. We cannot hoard nor can we waste any of His gifts foolishly. Neither can we honor the Lord by being a miser or a prodigal. We honor the Lord by acknowledging Him as the Author of every good and perfect gift and, praising Him for His goodness to us and giving thanks for His love and all that He has given us in Christ.

In Old Testament days a *tithe* of what one possessed was to be given back to the Lord. If in Old Testament days the tithe was required by law, how much more should be given under grace. It is impossible to out give God! Our giving to God keeps the windows of heaven open for Him to pour out new mercies every morning.

No selfish, stingy person can succeed. The rich farmer tried it and lost everything. "'God loves a cheerful giver" and the sooner we give God top priority in our lives, the sooner He withholds no good thing from those who walk uprightly. He *always* supplies our need and unless we share with others what He has so generously given to us, we become the losers. When we give, let us honor God in so doing. Let us see to it that our *motive* is good, that our *object* is good, and that our *proportion* is good.

> "Give, and it shall be given unto you,
> Good measure, pressed down,
> Shaken together, and running over."
> Luke 6:38

A Prayer Thought

Lord, help me to give willingly out of a heart full of love for You. May I never give grudgingly or out of necessity, but as a rejoicing, cheerful giver. As a steward of Yours, may I continually be grateful for what you have given to me. In return, may I freely give back to You Your portion and may I always freely and unselfishly give to those in need. In Christ's name I pray. Amen. (Matthew 10:8b)

Chapter Thirteen

THE PRINCIPLES OF REJOICING AND THANKFULNESS

We are told by the Psalmist, "Rejoice in the Lord, you righteous, and give thanks at the remembrance of His holiness" (Psalm 97:12). The Apostle Paul backs up this law in his writings. In Philippians he says, "Rejoice in the Lord always, and again I say rejoice" (4:4). And then in First Thessalonians he says, "In everything give thanks for this is the will of God in Christ Jesus concerning us" (5:18). By combining the words *rejoice* and *thanks*, God is telling us to "brighten up, be joyful and smile."

OUR REJOICING

The Word of God is filled with God's goodness and for His wonderful works to the children of men. He makes the sun to shine on the evil and the good and sends rain on the just and unjust alike. He has provided a salvation for every lost sinner. While the vast majority of people are on the broad road leading to destruction, those who have accepted Christ as their Savior are headed for glory and have cause for rejoicing.

The blessings God has bestowed upon those children who by faith have been born again are innumerable, resulting in our rejoicing as we celebrate this goodness on our behalf. This causes us to "Bless the Lord, O my soul, and forget not all His benefits" (Psalm 103:2). We rejoice and bless the Lord—

1. *For His Salvation.* "I have trusted in God's mercy. My heart shall rejoice in His salvation" (Psalm 13:5.)

2. *For His Redeeming Power.* "My lips shall greatly rejoice when I sing unto the Lord and for my soul, which has been redeemed" (Psalm 71:23).

3. *Because He made me righteous and glad for it.* "Let the righteous be glad, let them rejoice before God" (Psalm 68:3).

4. *For His Defense.* "Let all those who put their trust in the Lord rejoice, let them ever shout for joy, because God defends them. Let those who love His name be joyful in Him" (Psalm 5:11).

5. *For His Word.* "Holding forth [or clinging to] the Word of Life, that I may

rejoice in the day of Christ and not run in vain neither labor in vain" (Philippians 2:16). "I rejoice at God's Word as one who finds great treasure" (Psalm 119:152).

6. *When Christ is Preached.* In spite of divisions some were preaching Christ in pretense or envy, but Paul was grateful that "Christ is preached, and I therein rejoice, yea, and will rejoice" (Philippians 1:18).

7. *By Rejoicing Day by Day.* If the Lord spares us throughout the night and allows us to see the dawn of a new day. "This is the day which the Lord has made [the day He has appointed for whatever purpose He has in store for us], and we will be glad and rejoice in it" (Psalm 118:24). We do not know what the next day will hold for us, but we can thank God we know Who holds it. What a cause for rejoicing!

8. *For Trials.* "I will be glad and rejoice in God's mercy, for He has considered my troubles, He has made known my soul" (Psalm 31:7). "Beloved, think it not strange concerning the fiery trial which is to try you, as though some strange thing happened to you, but rejoice, inasmuch as you are partakers of Christ's sufferings, that, when His glory shall be revealed you may be glad also with exceeding joy" (I Peter 4:12,13).

9. *For our Hope.* "By faith in His grace we stand and rejoice in hope of the glory of God, for what is our hope, or our joy, or the Crown of Rejoicing. Are not even we in the presence of our Lord Jesus Christ at His coming?" (Romans 5:2; I Thessalonians 2:19).

10. *Because we shall see the Lord personally.* "Whom not having seen, we love. In whom, though now you see Him not, yet believing, we rejoice with joy unspeakable and full of glory" (I Peter 1:8). This joy is ours on this side of the Rapture. Because we are the children of God in Christ, "it does not appear what we shall be, but we know that when He appears, *we shall be like Him for we shall see Him as He is* (I John 3:2).

11. The Rapture of the Church. Having looked for that blessed hope and the glorious appearing of the great God and our Savior Jesus Christ, "Let us be glad and rejoice and give Him honor and glory, for the Marriage Supper of the Lamb is come and His wife, the Bride, has made herself ready" (Titus 2:13; Revelation 19:7).

Summary

On consideration of the benefits listing God's goodness to those who name His name, "Let us shout for joy and be glad, those who favor My righteous cause. Let them say continually, the Lord be magnified" (Psalm 35:27). No wonder Paul said, "Rejoice, *and again I say rejoice*" (Philippians 4:4).

Our Thankfulness

When we think of all the different blessings and benefits God has given us in which we can be glad and rejoice, the "Principle of Thanksgiving" appears upon the scene. "In *everything* give thanks, for this is the will of God in Christ Jesus concerning us" (I Thessalonians 5:18).

The early American Pilgrims had a well-rooted understanding of giving thanks to God. They patterned their celebration after the Biblical Festival of Tabernacles. Like the Israelites, they celebrated God's goodness and provisions. This feast was the last of the sacred festivals and was held at the close of the whole harvest and vintage to acknowledge the bounty of God in crowning the whole year with His blessings. It was designed to be a time of thanksgiving for God's protecting His people in their wilderness journey.[48]

For the believer *everyday* should be a time for thanksgiving—thanking the Lord for who He is and all that He has done and provided for us as pilgrims and strangers on earth. The Psalmist tells us "It is a good thing to give thanks unto the Lord" (92:1). Since we are required to give God thanks in everything, Scripture reminds us when we should do it. We are to "Stand every morning to thank and praise the Lord and likewise at evening" (I Chronicles 23:30). The Psalmist said "At midnight I will rise to give thanks unto God because of His righteous judgment" (119:62). The implication of these verses is similar to the verse that tells us to "Pray without ceasing." We are to give the Lord thanks without ceasing—always in an attitude of thanksgiving. Because we are to give our heavenly Father thanks in everything, let us begin with—

1. God's unspeakable Gift, the Lord Jesus Christ (II Corinthians 9:15). On the basis of what we know about Him from the Bible, there is much we can say in appreciation to God for Him. Here is a brief summary of:

Our Unique Savior[49]

Jesus Christ was born in the meanest of circumstances, but the air above was filled with the hallelujahs of a heavenly host. His lodging was an animal's pen but a star drew lowly shepherds from their fields to witness a Savior who had been born, an event they noised abroad.

His relatives were inconspicuous and uninfluential. In infancy He was recognized in the Temple as "salvation;" in boyhood He startled the doctors; in manhood He ruled the elements, defying the law of gravitation by walking on water and then quieting the raging sea. He healed multitudes without medicine and made no charge for His services. He never wrote a book, yet all the libraries in the world could not hold the books that have been written about Him. He never wrote a song, yet He has furnished the theme of more songs than all the song writers combined. He never founded a college, yet all the schools together cannot boast of as many students as He has. He never practiced medicine, yet he has healed more broken hearts than the doctors have broken bodies.

He never marshalled an army or drafted a soldier or fired a gun, yet no leader ever had more volunteers who have, under His orders, made rebels stack arms or surrender without a shot being fired.

He is the Harmonizer of all discords. Great men have come and gone, yet He lives on. Herod could not kill Him, Satan could not seduce Him, even demons obeyed Him. He had no cornfields or fisheries, but He could spread a table for about five thousand men and their families and have bread and fish to spare. He broke up every funeral He saw.

He had nothing He could call His own. The foxes have holes and the birds of the air have nests, but He had no place to lay His head. He was born in a borrowed stable, rode on a borrowed donkey, preached from another's boat, was nailed to another's cross, and was buried in a borrowed tomb.

His crucifixion was the crime of crimes, the innocent suffering for the guilty. When He died, few men mourned; but a black crepe was hung over the sun. Though men trembled not for their sins, the earth beneath shook under the load. All nature honored Him, sinners alone rejected Him. He forgave His enemies and loved those who hated His truth. He gave His life that others might live.

He is the only Perfect One—the only One who can satisfy the soul and give eternal life to sinners. He paid a debt He didn't owe because we had a debt we couldn't pay. Without Him we can do nothing—with Him we can do all things.

With the hymn writer we can say, "Hallelujah, what a Savior!" With these thoughts of God's unspeakable Gift and the life He lived among the human race, we can continue to give Him thanks—

2. For Christ finding us when we were lost (Luke 19:10).

3. For God the Father drawing us to Christ (John 6:44).

4. For the Holy Spirit convicting us of our sin, Christ's righteousness, and judgment to come if we do not repent and believe the Gospel (John 16:7–9).

5. For giving us the gift of faith to receive and believe on Christ for salvation (Ephesians 2:8,9; Galatians 2:16; John 1:12).

6. For elevating us from destruction—lifting us out of the miry clay, setting our feet upon "the Solid Rock" and giving us a song of praise (Psalm 40:2,3,5; 69:30).

7. For the blessing of coronation, crowning us with loving kindness and tender mercies (Psalm 103:4b,5a).

8. For satisfying us with good things and renewing our strength, delivering us from the power of darkness and translating us into the kingdom of God's dear Son (Psalm 103:5b; Colossians 1:13).[50] (points 6–8).

9. For giving us victory through Christ over our enemy, Satan, with the usage of God's whole armor (Ephesians 6:10–18; I Corinthians 10:13). This enables us to submit ourselves unto God, resist the devil who then will flee from us. We then become more than conquerors through Christ who loves us (James 4:7; Romans 8:37).

10. Throughout each day we must give thanks to God and praise Him for Christ's glorious name, Whom He has exalted with a name that is above every name (I Chronicles 29:13). We are to be thankful unto Him, bless His name and sing unto the Lord. We must never forget His wonderful name, the One to which every knee, sooner or later, will have to bow (Psalm 100; Philippians 2:9–11).

In spite of all the blessings from God we have considered and our obedience to the "Principle of Thanksgiving," there are a number of things we have to consider from the physical standpoint. The patriarch Job tells us that man comes forth like a flower and is cut down; he flees also as a shadow and continues not" (14:1,2). Job also said that "Man is born unto trouble as sparks fly upward" (5:7).

Even when we are born again, from that time 'till we either die or the Rapture takes place, a number of things can befall us. Old Job experienced quite a number of physical set-backs. We too, can suffer illness, pain, heartache, depression, fear, and anxiety. There could come a time when one feels all hope is gone and are on the verge of giving up. Some folks become bitter in the death of a loved one or if accident befalls them. To give thanks *in* everything as well as *for* everything is not the easiest thing to do (I Thessalonians 5:18; Ephesians 5:20). So often there are those who point an accusing finger at God when disaster strikes, even blaming Him for the catastrophe. We have to realize that God would never require our thanks *in* and *for* everything if He didn't have an out for us. There is someone out there who is in worse shape that we, whether we want to admit it or not.

Let us take the Apostle Paul for example. Just because he stood up for the Lord and preached Christ, he was imprisoned, whiplashed five times with forty stripes save one, and was beaten three times with rods. Once he was stoned and left for dead. He suffered shipwreck and floundered in the sea day and night. He was in perils of flood, in perils of robbers, in perils with his own countrymen [the Jews] and with the Gentiles (II Corinthians 11:23–27). He had no place tu live on his own, had to work with his hands, was reviled, persecuted, defamed, was made the filth [rubbish, scum] of the world and was despised (I Corinthians 4:11–13). On one occasion he had his clothes torn off, was beaten with many stripes and imprisoned. Bleeding and in pain, he and his partner, Silas, had a "singspiration" at midnight (Acts 16:22–25). Regardless of his lot, he could say, "For to me to live is Christ and to die is gain" (Philippians 1:21). What a testimony!

Old Job lost all his livestock and servants. A windstorm blew down the house of his sons and daughters and killed them. He was smitten with sore boils from the sole of his foot to the top of his head. Even his wife turned against him saying, "Curse God and die." In all of this Job did not sin (1:1–2:10). On two different occasions he said (1), "Naked I came out of my mother's womb and naked shall I depart. The Lord gave and the Lord has taken away, blessed be the name of the Lord" (1:21). (2) "Though He slay me, yet will I trust in Him: I will maintain my way before Him" (13:15). As a result of Job's faithfulness and his attitude of thankfulness for the Lord being with him through thick and thin, "the Lord blessed the latter end of Job more than his beginning with seven sons and three daughters, plus more livestock" (42:12,13).

Think for a moment about Jesus. He was ridiculed, threatened, scoffed at and despised by His own kinsmen. He was falsely tried and sentenced to die by the awful torture of crucifixion. He was crowned king with a crown of thorns, spat upon and scourged. Scourging was different, more painful than being whipped. In scourging, the whip had several thongs with sharp flint of bones at the end. Each lash not only tore the back to shreds but wrapped around the body injuring the chest. His hair was torn out by the roots and His visage was so marred He was hardly recognized. The back was a mass of bloody pulp upon which the cross was placed. Falling beneath it He staggered up to Calvary's hill among the hisses of the crowd. It was there the huge metal spikes were driven into His hands and feet, creating greater excruciating pain. In it all He could have called down twelve legions

(72,000) of angels to rescue Him but He was willing to do His Father's will and in dying for all sinners, He forgave those who were guilty of His death.

Christ had said the world hated Him and would hate His followers (John 15:18). Many believers have forfeited their lives in defense of their faith for the sake of the Gospel. There is a book titled "Fox's Book of Martyrs."which unfolds the story of many believers over the years who laid down their lives for the One who laid down His for theirs.

Regardless for anyone's cause for suffering, one can always find time to look up and thank God that their lot isn't what so many other believers have gone through. Bear with me as I tell you of an experience I had in the Spring of 1994. I was a traveling Evangelist and Bible teacher. Having some heart murmurs my doctor put me in the hospital. After giving me a catheterization, I was given a four heart by-pass. A vessel had been taken from my left leg for this operation. Known only to my wife at that time, the doctors almost lost me. Two days later, due to taking the vessel from my leg, my foot began to develop clots. Blood thinning medicine did no good so on the third day my left leg was amputated just above the knee. Due to the blood thinning medication, I almost bled to death. A week later, with pains in my stomach, I was given an exploratory operation and it was discovered my gall bladder had erupted. Again they almost lost me. Other complications stepped in and I was in the hospital for seventy two days.

I personally believe the Lord put me in this hospital for a purpose. I witnessed to every doctor, nurse and maid and had the privilege of leading two nurses to the Lord. Doctors aren't usually the easiest ones to reach but as I left, one doctor said, "Pastor Robert, I'm beginning to understand what faith means." 'Till this day I have never questioned the Lord nor have I complained one time. I have never asked Him "Why me, Lord?" To say "Why me, Lord" implies I wish what befell me would have happened to someone else.

I have learned, due to my faith in God "doing mysterious things His wonders to perform," to say, "*What, Lord*, do you want me to do and say under any and all circumstances?" After each operation and test I said "Thank You, Lord, You have left me on planet earth for a purpose." God gave me four verses that kept me in a mood to rejoice and constantly thank Him in and *for* this experience. Take notice of the usage of the word *all*, not part, but *all*, in the following verses.

The first is, "*All* things are of God" (II Corinthians 5:18). In our relationship with Christ, we are "bone of His bone and flesh of His flesh" (Ephesians 5:39). Nothing happens to us but what it goes through Him first. He has borne our griefs and sorrows, taken our infirmities and borne our sicknesses (Isaiah 53:4; Matthew 8:17).

Second, all things are for *my* sake that the abundant grace might through my thanksgiving rebound to the glory of God" (II Corinthians 4:15). No matter what comes my way from the hand of God, it is for my sake—my good, to help me be drawn closer to the Lord and to be more dependent upon Him. This enables me no matter what I do in word and deed, to do all in the name of the Lord Jesus, giving thanks through Him to God the Father" (Colossians 4:17).

Third, "*All* things [no matter what] work together for *my* good because I love

The Principles of Rejoicing and Thankfulness 121

the Lord my God and because I have been called according to His purpose" (Romans 8:28). And what is His purpose for my life? "That I might be conformed to the image of His dear Son" (Romans 8:29). Each believer has a treasure in his earthen vessel (body) for the purpose of God's power to be manifested in us. We may be troubled on every side, yet not distressed. We still have room to breathe! We may be perplexed or puzzled, but never in despair. We may be persecuted but never left friendless nor forsaken by God. We may be knocked down but never knocked out. We always bear in our bodies the dying of the Lord Jesus so that the life of Jesus might be made manifest in our bodies. For we who live are always delivered unto death (of self) for Jesus' sake, that His life may be made visible in our mortal bodies (II Corinthians 4:7–11). We are to live so that others might take knowledge that we have been with Jesus. This is what I sought to do in the hospital, and with witnessing and giving out tracts, I had the happy, thankful privilege of leading two to the Lord.

Fourth. The Lord perfects or accomplishes *all* those things which concern or happens to us (Psalm 138:8). I believe this is why the Lord put me in the hospital. Thankfully, I can still drive, and do some preaching locally, even though I have to "sit down on the job" in my wheel chair. I have the privilege of visiting others who need cheering up and because so many friends were praying for me while in the hospital, I now spend more time praying for others. I am grateful the Lord gave me the privilege of giving Him thanks *in* and *for* everything that came my way.

CONCLUSION

As we look back at all the Apostle Paul went through, he taught us a great lesson when he said, "I have in whatsoever state I am, therewith to be content" (Philippians 4:11). We are to let our manner of life (behavior) be without covetousness and be content with such things as we have (Hebrews 13:5). It is only when we are so familiar with the Word of God and its influence in our lives that we walk hand in hand with Him. In this close relationship we are able to take every thing in stride, "on the chin." It matters not what, even though we may feel we have been pushed to the edge, we are not alone. Our Shepherd always walks with us, even in the valley of the shadow of death. With His presence by our side, we have a peace that passes all understanding. No matter our lot, we can fulfill the will of God by giving thanks for everything.

Thanksgiving Perspectives[51]
  —Its *Meaning*. The Hebrew word for "thanksgiving" conveys the extension of an open hand as it offers a sacrifice of adoration to God. The Greek word described worship offered through a grateful language from the heart.
  —Its *Application*. To give self to God with an open hand as a symbol of humility, indication, "I am withholding *nothing* from Him. You, God, have my all."
  —Its *Purpose*. To be thankful unto God and bless His name (Psalm

100:4). To magnify God, praising His name with song and thanksgiving, (Psalm 69:30), we make known His name and deeds among all people (I Chronicles 16:8; Deuteronomy 28:9,10).

—Its *Method*. In the offering of the sacrifice of thanksgiving, it must be offered of our own free will *with* song (Leviticus 22:29; Psalm 5:11).

—Thanking God must be a daily practice in the morning and in the evening (I Chronicles 23:30).

—We must thank God *in* and *for* everything (I Thessalonians 5:18; Ephesians 5:20)

—We must thank Him with full confidence, being anxious for nothing (Philippians 4:6).

Looking back at all the Scripture we have considered in this Chapter, things that cause rejoicing and all the things for which we can give thanks, let us summerize many things God's unspeakable gift, His only begotten Son, the Lord Jesus Christ, did for His redeemed ones—

Christ for Me[52]

He died (Matthew 27:50) that I might live (John 3:15).

He became poor that I might become rich (II Corinthians 8:9).

He suffered hunger (Matthew 4:2) that I might be satisfied with the "Bread of Life" (John 6:51).

He suffered thirst (John 19:28) that I might be fully and forever satisfied with the Water of Life (John 4:14; Revelation 7:16)

He was lonely (John 6:55) that I might never be alone (Matthew 28:20).

He was weary (John 4:6) that I might have rest (Matthew 11:28–30).

He was exceedingly sorrowful (Matthew 26:38) that I might have joy (John 15:11).

He was tempted (Matthew 4:1) that I might be delivered from the hour of temptation (I Corinthians 10:13).

He was forsaken (Matthew 26:56) that I may never be forsaken (Hebrews 13:5).

He was falsely accused and misrepresented (Luke 23:13,14) that I might have Him as a Friend Who understands and sticks closer than a brother (Hebrews 4:15,16; Proverbs 18:24).

He took upon Himself the form of man (Philippians 2:7) that I might be conformed to His image (Romans 8:29; Psalm 17:15).

He became a servant (Philippians 2:7) that I might become a son of God (John 1:12; I John 3:1).

He was separated from His Father (Matthew 27:46) that I might spend eternity with Him (I Thessalonians 4:16–18).

He suffered the wrath of God (Isaiah 53:3–11) that I might know the love of God (I John 4:10).

He endured the cross (Luke 23:33) that I might wear a crown (I Peter 5:4),

The Principles of Rejoicing and Thankfulness 123

He endured darkness (Matthew 27:45) that I might be called into His marvelous light (John 12:46; (I Peter 2:9b).

He was stripped of His robe (Matthew 27:31,35) that I might wear His robe of righteousness (Philippians 3:9; Revelation 19:7,8).

He wept (John 11:35) that God might wipe away all my tears (Revelation 21:4).

He was troubled (John 12:27) that I might have a peace that passes all understanding (Philippians 4:7)

He suffered persecution (Luke 4:28,29) that I might be of good cheer (John 16:31).

He was despised (Isaiah 53:3) that I might be exalted (Revelation 3:21).

He became an outcast (Matthew 8:20) that I might be welcomed (Revelation 22:17)

He became homeless in His own country (Luke 4:24) that I might have a home in glory with Him (John 14:1–3).

SUMMARY

In considering all that God through Christ has done for lost mankind and the blessings and new mercies He bestows upon His children each morning, how can any child of His not be rejoicing and thankful. What a pity it is for those who do not obey the Principle of Thanksgiving. What a tragedy they rob themselves of what God withholds from them because of their disobedience God has given us—[53]

—A *Life* that can never be forfeited.
—A *Relation* that can never be abolished.
—A *Righteousness* that can never be tarnished.
—An *Acceptance* that can never be questioned.
—A *Standing* that can never be disputed.
—A *Justification* that ca~ never be reversed.
—A *Seal* that can never be broken.
—An *Inheritance* that can never be alienated.
—A *Wealth* that can never be depleted.
—A *Possession* that can never be measured.
—A *Salvation* that can never be annulled.
—A *Forgiveness* that can never be rescinded.
—A *Grace* that can never be arrested.
—A *Strength* that can never be weakened or exhausted.
—An *Assurance* that can never be disappointed.
—An *Attraction* that can never be superceded.
—A *Comfort* that can never be lessened.
—A *Service* that will always be rewarded.
—An *Intercessor* Who can never be disqualified.
—A *Hope* that can never fade away.
—A *Glory* that will outshine the stars forever.

None dare say that God has not done His part, *and more too*! The least we can do as we rejoice and give thanks is, "Count Our Many Blessings, Name them *Ton* by Ton!"

"Were the whole realm of nature mine,
That were a present far too small;
Love so amazing so Divine,
Demands my soul, my life, my all!"[54]

A Prayer Thought

Dear heavenly Father, may my first thought in the morning be "thank You Lord for safety of the night." May my second one be "thank You Lord for the dawn of this new day." May my third one be "thank You Lord for faith in Your guidance throughout all the day, and may my last thought at night be "thank You Lord for Your unspeakable Gift, my wonderful Savior, Jesus Christ, and the home you have reserved for me in heaven. In His name I pray, Amen. (II Corinthians 9:15; I Peter 1:3–9)

Chapter Fourteen

THE PRINCIPLE OF THE CHRISTIAN'S WARFARE

The Apostle Paul reminds the believer that during his Christian life on earth, his weapons are not carnal, but mighty through God to the pulling down of strongholds (II Corinthians 10:4). God has provided each believer with His whole armor for our engagement in battle against our enemy, Satan. The *Principle* involved in this battle is "To put on this armor of God" (Ephesians 6:11a).

One of the reasons God leaves us here on earth when we are saved is for us to go through His *training camp* and learn lessons that will make heaven all the more precious. When we were saved God did not promise us a life of ease. We live in an evil world which is our battle field. Although we are blessed with God's love and the blessings of His promises, we are faced daily with the enemy of our souls, Satan himself, and his heavy artillery. Just as God has two wills for each human being, so does Satan. God's are (1) that each is saved, that none perish (II Peter 3:9), and (2) that each accepts Christ as his/her own personal Savior and live for Him on a daily basis, totally dedicated to our enduring hardness as good soldiers of Christ (II Timothy 2:3,4; II Corinthians 5:17). Satan's two wills are (1) to keep sinners blinded to the light of the glorious Gospel of Christ (II Corinthians 4:4), and (2) to keep those who accept Christ as *babes in Christ*, stunting their spiritual growth and causing them to live worldly lives (I Corinthians 3:1). God has no place for cowards in His army.

Why is Paul outlining the need for preparation in their warfare? Why do you, I, need to be qualified for battle?

1. We face tests daily.
2. Tasks must be performed daily.
3. We must make sure our emotional life is stable.
4. Our testimony must be unstained, unwavering, which will enable us to stand for God in any circumstance.
5. We must be mentally, morally and spiritually awake to all situations so that we can be a better witness for the Lord.

6. We must be so knowledgeable of God's Word to stand for the Lord and refute Satan as Christ did in the desert (Matthew 4:1–11).

With all the experiences Paul had with Satan, he was well aware of the fitness with which we must be equipped. Sadly the average child of God is not equipped to meet the enemy and his cohorts when the test comes. This is seen by the number of those who have joined ranks with the false teaching of cult leaders of today. Many of them were at one time good members of good fundamental Churches, but they failed to be clothed with God's whole armor. They were defeated time and time again and now have a bad spirit, a critical attitude, become easily offended, turn against the fundamental truths of God's Word and fall prey to Satan's devices. To qualify for becoming a good soldier, we must be Bereans—searching the Scriptures daily. Being rooted and grounded in the Word helps us to escape deception, avoid defeat and enjoy victory.

The good soldier is able "to stand against the wiles of Satan" (Ephesians 6:11). To stand has a two-fold meaning. 1. We must be aware—not ignorant of his devices. 2. "Stand" carries with it the thought of a candlestick, tall, and straight. When Jesus spoke of a lighted candle, He said men do not put it under a bushel, but on a candlestick and it gives a light to all in the house. Then He instructs the believer to let his light so shine that others might see your good works (Matthew 5:15,16). A bright light will blind the person who approaches us, and by our *stand*, we can oppose Satan's wiles, which are his craftiness, lies, cunning devices, error and temptations.

Satan's wiles can disturb the mind, deceive the heart and bring defeat into the life of the believer. He drew Lot into Sodom. He drove Abraham into Egypt and caused him to give a half truth about his wife, Sarah. He even got Aaron to build an idol, the golden calf, for Israel to worship.

He was pleased in getting Peter to deny Christ three times. He works hard to bring division in the Church, paralyze its ministry and bring slander to its members. He even dared to attack Christ. Don't you ever think you are immune to "that old serpent, the devil." We must ever be on guard, stand and let our light shine.

In our preparation for a battle, we must be knowledgeable of the enemy we are to encounter. We are not in a physical battle, but a spiritual one. We wrestle not against flesh and blood but against rulers of world forces of darkness and against spiritual forces of wickedness in heavenly places (Ephesians 6:12). Notice the word *wrestle*. It has to do with one man gripping another and straining every muscle to bring his opponent to a fall on the mat, and at the same time using every ounce of strength to resist defeat. This we are to do with our foe, whether false apostles, deceitful workers who transform themselves into servants of Christ, Satan himself or his emissaries—human or demonic (II Corinthians 11:13–15).

The Whole Armor of God (Ephesians 6:10–17)

To be more than a conqueror through Christ who loves us (Romans 8:37), as a good soldier, we must obey the command to "Put on the whole [not part but whole] armor of God." No one can fight the battle but you. You have to stand alone, yet not alone because if God be for us who can be against us (Romans 8:31b). This is *your* battle, your private battle. You will face the *world*, the *flesh* and the *devil*. There will be no let up. It will not be a skirmish. Satan will come in like a flood at any time. He has been in business for over 6,000 years on earth and he neither sleeps nor slumbers. But if we are dressed in God's whole armor, as the following points being out, God will make an avenue of escape from Satan's wiles and temptations so that we may be able to bear it (I Corinthians 10:13). We must keep in mind why Paul realized the need to constantly wear God's whole armor. God had permitted him to have a "thorn in the flesh," which was a messenger of Satan sent to buffet him. As a result, he was plagued with infirmities, reproach, persecution, distress [even opposition], but he accepted it all for Jesus' sake (II Corinthians 2:7,10). His example should challenge us to stand and utilize our whole armor and *keep* it on. This uniform is what the "well dressed" Christian soldier wears.

1. Truth (6:14a). The Roman soldier wore an ornamental belt. The Christian soldier girds his loins with the *truth* of God, the Gospel of Jesus Christ. Unless truth is known and contentiously believed no man can enter the spiritual warfare with any advantage or prospect of success. By truth alone we discover who our enemies are and what their plan of attack is. By truth we know where our strength lies, hence we gird ourselves with this strength to stand against all false religions and any winds of false doctrines which cunning men and treacherous demons of Satan use to deceive. Truth may at times be taken for granted and if a believer is not aware that his heart is not right before God, in vain will he anticipate victory. This piece of armor—truth—is what sets us free, free from the one who had us bound in sin (John 8:32). Truth stands for the "power of God unto salvation for all who believe, to the Jew first and also to the Gentiles" (Romans 1:16). Truth is the only weapon against the untruth Satan propagates.

2. Breastplate of Righteousness (6:14b). The word righteousness conveys several meanings—

1. It signifies the *principle* of righteousness.
2. It signifies the *practice* of righteousness—or living a holy life.
3. It signifies God's *method* of justifying sinners.
4. It signifies *justification* itself.[55]

The breastplate protects the heart, assuring us that our belief in God's truth will be sufficient to be the victor. It also carries with it the thought that we must daily practice in our lives the holiness of God—full dedication, a complete sacrifice of self. Satan cringes when he takes notice that God's soldier is permitting God to conform him to Christ's image. Not only does the breastplate defend the heart, but the lungs and all the other vital parts that are contained from the neck to the abdomen (thorax). The first two pieces of armor—loins gird about with truth and the breastplate, give protection from the neck down to the loins.

3. Feet Shod with the Gospel (6:15). Shod feet were considered very important. Looseness of sandals would cause a slow walk, hinder a march, or injure the feet. If the feet were injured as soldier could neither stand to resist the enemy nor flee from him. The word *shod* played an essential role in marching and pursuing the enemy. "Shod" means a sole bound under the foot, with the thought of keeping the shoes on so that at a moment's notice soldiers would be ready to march. To shod a horse means to literally nail the shoe to the horse's hoof, making it a part of the horse. The Gospel is a part of each believer, not something to be kicked off after the Sunday Church service and not put on again till next Sunday. Being shod with the preparation of the Gospel of peace means *habitual readiness* to follow in the footsteps of Jesus, always ready to witness of the good news of salvation, in season and out of season. If we confess Christ, He will confess us before His Father who is in heaven. If we don't, Satan is the victor and Christ will not confess us before His Father (Matthew 10:32,33). He who has his feet shod with the Gospel of peace has beautiful feet wherever he goes, and is a victorious soldier for the cause of Christ (Isaiah 52:7; Romans 10:15).

4. The Shield of Faith (6:16). Faith is the most important defensive weapon, for without faith it is impossible to please God (Hebrews 11:6). Faith makes it possible to win and be rewarded by God. Faith here is represented as a huge shield to protect the whole body. It enables us to have full trust in the Lord. With faith we are protected from unseen things which could sneak up on us to strike a damaging blow. In ancient warfare bowmen were vital on the front line of battle to shoot their arrows at their enemy. Their arrows had fiery darts to burn or sting long enough to cause one to or enable the enemy to come in for the kill. With faith in God we believe He goes before us to fight our battles, enabling our shield of faith to ward off these fiery darts. Even though the shield is large we can "peep" over the top to keep an eye of the foe.

5. The Helmet of Salvation (6:17a). Ancient helmets had on the peak a figure that symbolized strength, such as a winged lion or some imaginary monster. The Apostle Paul probably referred to one that had the emblematic representation of a "helmet with the *hope* of salvation (I Thessalonians 5:8). With a hope of continual safety and protection, built upon the promises of God, and possessing the mind of Christ (I Corinthians 2:16), our helmet protects our mind to the point that our understanding is not darkened nor will it be confused by the temptations of the devil. We have the promise that God will "make a way of escape for us in any temptation that comes our way (I Corinthians 10:13). Ancient helmets were so hard that no matter how many sword or axe blows were given, each would glance off, enabling the soldier to keep fighting. Satan might attack us with all the powerful rulers of darkness but even though he might hedge us in, we can still breathe. He might cause us to suffer embarrassment or become perplexed, but he cannot drive us to despair. He may persecute us but God will never leave us nor forsake us. Satan may even knock us down but thank God He can never knock us out! God permits all this so that we might bear in our bodies the dying of Jesus Christ. His death works in us so that as we win, His life might work in others (II Corinthi-

The Principle of the Christian's Warfare

ans 4:7–12). I once heard a preacher say, "He who has Christ in his heart cannot be cheated out of the hope of victory, nor can he ever be cheated out of the hope of his eternal home in heaven."

The weapons of God's armor we have discussed so far—*Truth*, *Breastplate* of Righteousness, *Feet shod* with the preparation of the Gospel, the *Shield* of Faith and the *Helmet* of Salvation, all of which are *defensive* weapons for the body. The next weapon is our *offensive* weapon.

6. The Sword of the Spirit, which is the Word of God (6:17b). As the sword was the ancient soldier's weapon, so God's Word is our only offensive weapon. It is more powerful than any of Satan's, as Christ proved when He was tempted in the wilderness (Matthew 4:1–11). In a sense we are to use it as a defensive weapon to ward off Satan's attacks and offensively to help destroy his strategies. God's Word is quick and powerful, and sharper than any two-edged sword, piercing even to the dividing asunder of soul and spirit and of the joints and marrow, and is a discerner of the heart (Hebrews 4:12). Try as hard as he can, Satan is no match for Scripture. He deceived Eve by twisting it, but his deception caught up with him (Genesis 3:1–15).

By faith, as we take the "sword," the unchanging Word of God, it immediately becomes our assurance which enables us to stand firm in the liberty Christ has given to us. As we submit ourselves to the Lord the devil will flee from us as we resist him (James 4:7). What was good for Christ to trick the devil with each time he tempted Him, is good enough for us. An old country preacher once said, "There are two things the old devil can't stand and the Word of God is both of them!"

Praying Always (6:18). Having considered the fact that when one accepts Christ as Savior—is born again by the Spirit of God—from this point on till he meets the Lord face to face, he is on the battle field as one of God's soldiers. In considering the stand he must take and his being clad in God's whole armor he must wear in combat, Paul does not include *prayer* as a part of the armor, but with the necessity of the soldier's equipment, he reveals the importance of prayer. Prayer is definitely needed to keep the "Principle of Our Warfare." Without it we cannot successfully resist those principalities and powers, the rulers of darkness and wickedness, and even Satan himself. The Apostle shows that God's warriors must depend upon the "Captain of our salvation" and pray always as we depend upon Him and Him alone Who can defeat the tactics of our vile enemy and give victory. Satan may be a sergeant but Christ as Captain ranks higher than a sergeant. Having given allegiance to our Captain, we must obey when He gives orders.

Prayer is needed to encourage and fortify soldiers of the Cross never to retreat, never to turn their backs on the Lord and run from Satan when they think he might be getting the upper hand. The armor protects the *front* of the body as we are following the Lord with Satan trying to come in between. To turn our back on the Lord and run from Satan, we expose ourselves to him with no protection.

There *is* power in prayer. Our prayer life shows our dependence upon the Lord and this could be one reason Paul said to *pray always*. On another occasion he said to *pray without ceasing* (I Thessalonians 5:17). These expressions do not mean we are to constantly pray twenty-four hours a day, but to be so in tune with the Lord that at a moment's notice we are on speaking terms with Him, that we can contact Him immediately. "The effectual fervent prayer of a righteous man avails much" (I Peter 5:16b).

"Watch and pray" means we watch our enemy, observing every move of his, and at the same time pray and look to God for His answer. No matter our situation with that old serpent the devil, we can endure hardness as a good soldier of Jesus Christ by using God's armor, standing up for Him, and being backed up with fervent prayer. In each instance by obeying God's Principle we always will be the victor (Romans 8:37). Prayer is a golden river at whose brink some die of thirst, while others kneel and drink. God help us to pray always.

Paul adds to the expression *praying always* "with all prayer and supplication in the Spirit and with this view, be on the alert with all perseverence and supplication for all saints" (6:18). "The expression *in the Spirit* means surrendering to God's will to assure us that He is with us. As we *persevere* we "hang in there," never giving up. *Supplication* deals with different things we must pray for during the course of individual battles. *Always* has to do with constantly being in an attitude of prayer. *For all saints* means to remember you are not the only soldier in your Company. Just as others pray for us, we must pray for others in our battalion."[56]

As we become engaged in battle, the power of prayer fortifies us as we stand for the Lord. In this warfare, we stand—

> In the faith: I Corinthians 16:13.
> In His grace: Romans 5:2.
> In the Gospel: I Corinthians 15:1.
> In the freedom of liberty: Galatians 5:1.
> In the Lord: Philippians 4:1.
> In one spirit and one mind: Philippians 1:27.
> Perfect and complete in the will of God; Colossians 4:12.
> For good in evil days: Ephesians 6:13.
> Against the wiles of Satan: Ephesians 6:11.

As we make prayer a part of our lives on a daily basis, we can stand in the power of His might (Ephesians 6:10). "If we don't stand for something we are liable to fall for anything" (Peter Marshall).

Our Body, the Temple of God

In Old Testament times God dwelt in the Tabernacle and in the Temples of Solomon, Zerubbabel's after Israel's Babylonian captivity, and Herod's Temple which existed during Christ's day. God's Temple today is the body of the believer, His House of Prayer. It is no wonder He protects it with His whole armor (I Corinthians 3:16; II Corinthians 6:19,20).

As Jesus cleaned out God's House of Prayer, the Temple, our House of Prayer must be kept clean so the glory of the Lord can shine forth. "We are not only soldiers in the battle field but we are "janitors" who must work full time so that we

The Principle of the Christian's Warfare 131

will have our heavenly Father's approval when He inspects His Temple. Because God dwells in my body, I meet Him and commune with Him in continual fellowship. I am at liberty to pray unto Him at anytime, without ceasing, always. I trust Him for help in finding the escape route when I face temptations because He is faithful and has promised never to leave or forsake me.

"This House of Prayer, God's House, that I maintain must be kept holy because it is holy. To defile it offends God, grieves the Holy Spirit and brings disgrace to Christ. He must "chase out" any evil by chastisement and as we confess and forsake out sin, He forgives us and cleanses us. Living by the Spirit makes us condemnation free."[57] This certainly will lessen our janitorial work! (Proverbs 28:13; I John 1:9).

Pay Day—Rewards

One last thought. There is always a "pay day" for the soldiers. When a child of God endures hardness as a good soldier of Jesus Christ and overcomes temptation with all the equipment God has provided for victory, each victory will help win another. A triumph today will help gain another victory tomorrow. Triumph is the joy of the believer. In the service of the Lord, they are building upon the foundation Jesus Christ gold, silver and precious stones, valuable rewards for faithful service (I Corinthians 3:11,12a). Pay day takes place at the judgment seat of Christ immediately following the Rapture of the Church (I Thessalonians 4:16,17). And what is the "pay" or rewards for their undying faithful service as a good soldier?

1. A *Crown of Life* for enduring temptations or trials (James 1:12). The good soldier lives an exemplary life before God and others. In his stand for his Captain, God provides a way of escape from a temptation so that he may be able to overcome it (I Corinthians 10:13).

2. *An Incorruptible Crown* for their not turning to the left nor to the right but faithfully staying on course (I Corinthians 9:24,25; Joshua 1:7).

3. A *Crown of Glory* for being true to the Word of God, standing up to Satan and rebuffing him with the "sword of the spirit," which is the inspired Word of God (I Peter 5:1–4; Matthew 4:1–11; II Timothy 3:16,17).

4. A *Crown of Rejoicing* for being true to Christ's admonition that His children must be His witnesses in giving the plan of salvation to sinners and winning them to the Lord (I Thessalonians 2:19,20; Acts 1:8; Psalm 107:2; Proverbs 11:30; Daniel 12:3).

5. A *Crown of Rejoicing*. This crown is reserved for all those who look for the coming of Jesus Christ—who love His appearing at the Rapture (II Timothy 4:8). The believer, in looking for Christ's return perseveres faithfully, or continually abides in Christ so that when He appears, he will not be ashamed before Him at His coming (I John 2:28). And thankfully, when we see Jesus, we shall be as He is. This hope of His coming and becoming Like Him is a challenge to keep ourselves purified, even as He is pure (I John 3:2,3).

There are other rewards given to mature believers such as one for our faithfulness to the Lord (Ruth 2:12), one for enduring persecution (Matthew 5:11,12), one for using our God given talents (Matthew 25:19–23), and one for performing insignificant deeds, such as giving a cup of cold water to the thirsty in the name of the Lord (Mark 9:41).

"Our motive for receiving rewards should not be a selfish one, but that we might have these precious items to lay at the feet of Jesus in appreciation for all He did for us and the provisions He made for us to faithfully follow Him (Revelation 4:10,11). What a tragedy to be in heaven empty-handed! Better to have it said 'saved by grace' than 'saved yet so as by fire' (I Corinthians 3:13–15). Better to have the blessed Savior say 'Well done good and faithful servant' than to have to stand there and see works, due to lack of faithfulness, burned and suffer loss. The fact that the Lord Himself is our 'Reward' (Genesis 15:1) is good enough for any believer to be a faithful servant, walking uprightly day by day, moment by moment. The believer who so walks, God will withhold no good thing from him" (Psalm 84:11)[58]

CONCLUSION
Resolve to Face Your Enemy[59]

Will you follow Jesus or be swayed by the message of your enemy and the message of the world? Once you make the decision to follow Christ you must learn to rehearse His truth, which is the Word of God. Study it, memorize it, and pray that God will show you how to apply His Scripture to your life each day. Realize the Word of God [clothed with His whole armor, backed up with prayer] is your victorious weapon to your life each day. Realize His Word [the sword of the Spirit], is your [offensive] and victorious weapon against the enemy's deadly schemes. Renounce all unholy thoughts [and bring into captivity *every* thought to the obedience of Christ and ignore all disobedience when your obedience is fulfilled: II Corinthians 10:5,6]. When God views your life, He sees the life of His Son and the potential that is there. Be ready for the battle and remember you are God's beloved child. He will grant the victory for the trial you are facing when you place your trust in Him.

A Prayer Thought

Dear Lord, first I want to say thanks for Your goodness to me in making every provision to be more than a "conqueror" through Christ. Please help me to have continual recognition of Your presence in my body, to totally rely upon the Holy Spirit's power and guidance and all the resources that come from Your Word to protect me. Keep me mindful of Satan's power and may I always be mindful that "if You are for me," no one can be against me. In Jesus' name I pray. Amen.   (Psalm 145:18–21; Hebrews 11:6)

Chapter Fifteen

THE PRINCIPLE OF JUDGMENT

"Prepare to meet God," and "It is appointed unto man once to die and after that the judgment" (Amos 4:12b; Hebrews 9:27). Scripture mentions four judgments. Two are present and two are future. Tragically, very little is said today from pulpits across America about God's present judgment and upon death the judgment of hell—a Christless eternity. Liberals either deny it or air-condition it. Hell is just another by-word to many people. They think all they will get is here on earth.

Before we get into a discussion of these four judgments, let us consider a Biblical background of God's "so great salvation" that goes from Genesis through Revelation like a "scarlet thread." It begins with the promise of a Messiah, the Lord Jesus Christ in Genesis 3: 15 and goes all the way through Scripture to Jesus as the "Bright and Morning Star" Who is the "Alpha and Omega, the beginning and the ending, the first and the last" (Revelation 23:13,16).

Two words stand out in relation to salvation—*faith* and *righteousness*, both of which give us standing with God. Although the two words are not always mentioned in relation to this bond with God, the implication is there and we can see it in many instances. Adam and Eve had to accept by faith the "coats of skin" to be received back into fellowship with God. So did Abel, Seth, Enoch and Noah. Noah was called a "preacher of righteousness" so that man by faith would be right with God in view of the impending flood (II Peter 2:5). Noah and his family were called into the ark because of their righteousness (Genesis 7:1). Abraham's faith was counted for righteousness (Genesis 15:6). We find that the Gospel was preached to the Israelites. Faith on their part was required to possess salvation but they failed to exercise it (Hebrews 4:2). Throughout the prophecies relating to Christ, it is evident people heard enough truth about salvation because the prophets searched the Scriptures diligently for a fuller understanding of the Gospel that came by the grace of God (I Peter 1:10).

As we come into the New Testament period, even under the preaching of the Gospel by none other than Jesus Christ Himself, many were called but few heeded his message (Matthew 20:16b). Even though Christianity took hold in the first century, there was much opposition by the majority of people. Jesus told us that "many are on the broad road leading to destruction and only a few are on the straight and narrow way that leads to eternal life (Matthew 7:13,14). Let us consider first—

1. The Judgment of Sinners

God's first judgment upon the human race began with Adam and Eve. When Adam sinned, his sin of disobedience passed upon all humans, making them sinners by nature (Romans 5:12; 19a). Having accepted God's provision of "coats of skin" from an animal sacrifice, they were expelled from the Garden of Eden. After the birth of Cain and Abel, Abel's faith was counted for righteousness in the sacrifice he offered and "he being dead, yet speaks" (Genesis 4:1–4; Hebrews 11:4). Self-righteous Cain's offering was an offering of works. God gave him opportunity to repent and offer an acceptable sacrifice in faith but he refused. In anger, he killed Abel and his judgment was greater than he could bear. He was driven out from the presence of God (Genesis 4:5–16). His self-righteous sacrifice and his act of anger has followed him 'till this day. Jude says "woe unto those who go the way of Cain" (vs. 11).

As history progressed, only a few are mentioned who wholly followed the Lord. Seth, who replaced Abel, and his descendants began to call upon the name of the Lord (Genesis 4:24,26). His descendants, through the patriarch Noah, maintained a good testimony for the Lord (Genesis 5:6–32).

The vast majority of people refused to listen to the testimony of God's obedient children and by the time of Noah's day and the flood, approximately 1,600 years had passed. We learn that prior to the flood God saw the wickedness of man, that every imagination of their hearts was evil continually. Although the Spirit of God strove with all these sinners, they ignored the preaching of righteousness by Noah. God's judgment was poured out of them by a world-wide flood (Genesis 6:3,5–7; II Peter 2:5). Only Noah and his family were spared.

After the flood there is a long history throughout the Old Testament of God's judgment upon sinners. After the sons of Noah settled in northern, southern and eastern areas, and the population increased, again the vast majority sought to "do that which was right in their own eyes." Due to there being one language at that time, a group got together to "get to heaven on their own." They started building a tower to make a name for themselves in case they were threatened by a flood again. This act of self-righteousness and works brought God's judgment upon them and by confusing their tongues into separate languages, they were scattered abroad (Genesis 11:1–9).

During Israel's wilderness journey, due to the majority living in unbelief and murmuring against God, they suffered the judgment of death. (Numbers 14:26–30). The sons of Korah and their followers rebelled against God's leaders, Moses and Aaron. They were then judged by an act of nature—an earthquake which swallowed all of them and their families. They went down alive into the pit—sheol or hell (Numbers 16:1–5,31–33 with Isaiah 14:15).

Suffice it to say there are many more illustrations we could refer to in the Old Testament. We can summarize them by saying that as a result of rejecting

The Principle of Judgment

God's plan of salvation, the end result was the "pit" or hell. The word hell is referred to thirty-two times in the Old Testament, mentioning the place where unbelievers go. See Second Peter 2:4–6; Jude 5–19.

As we approach the New Testament we find a greater emphasis is placed upon the place God has provided for Christ rejecters. There is a reason for this. There are only two places people can go after death—heaven or hell. One of the purposes of Christ's death was to make an avenue of escape from hell and to give believers in Him a place in heaven. It is a most important subject and should be emphasized over and over, just like we should emphasize the remedy to escape it. It should be preached whether people like it or not. Sinners need to be reminded that they are condemned and under God's wrath (John 3:18,36). "The heathen sink down into the pit" (Psalm 9:15).

As loving and compassionate as Jesus was in His preaching, He was the greatest "hell fire and brimstone" preacher that ever lived. He preached three times more on this subject than He did on heaven! He wanted to warn people of their doom if they rejected Him. I believe He also wanted to challenge His followers to witness more to win more to an acceptance of the Gospel (Ezekiel 3:17–19).

We need to look at some instances when He referred to this place. There were times He made direct statements. He told His hearers to fear the One who was able to sentence to death both soul and body in hell, namely God (Matthew 10:28). He spoke of the worldly inhabitants of Capernaum being brought down to hell (Matthew 11:23). He told the hypocritical Scribes and Pharisees it was impossible for them to escape the damnation of hell (Matthew 23:33). He spoke of hell by usage of allusion, saying that if a hand caused one to sin, better to cut the hand off and go through life maimed than go to hell with two hands (Mark 9:43). He also gave a historical reference of an unbeliever. In Luke 16 He mentioned a rich man who died and went to hell (or *hades*, the equivalent of *sheol* in the Old Testament). He was in torment and cried unto Abraham to have mercy on him. Being tormented in a flame he requested some water to cool him (vss. 19–26).

On one occasion when I had a visit from an insurance salesman, he vividly described the need of insurance for automobile accidents, bodily injury and death; house fires and loss of everything; sickness and out of work, etc. His emphasis was on all I could lose. The cost of it all was staggering. When he finished I said, "O.K., sir, I've listened to your sales pitch, now listen to mine. I, too, am an insurance salesman, but my policy has to do with the spiritual. Yours was to the physical. I then began to unfold what he could lose—his own soul—and where his final resting place would be—hell. I began to describe the place where he would spend all eternity, letting him know that hell is a—[60]

 —Flame of fire: Luke 16:24.
 —Furnace of fire: Matthew 13:42.
 —Lake of fire: Revelation 20:15.
 —Place of darkness: Matthew 8:12; II Peter 2:4; Jude 13.
 —Place of sorrows: Psakfl 18:5.
 —Place of torment: Luke 16:24.

—Place of filth: Revelation 21:8.
—Place where the worm dies not, where the fire is not quenched. It is everlasting (Matthew 25:41; Mark 9:43; Revelation 14:11). I told him my policy was free; it was God's gift to him because of Christ's death in his behalf as a sinner. He seemed concerned but sadly *no sale* (Romans 6:23).

Who are the inhabitants of hell? Satan and his demons will be there (Matthew 25:41). Fallen angels will be there (Jude 6). All the wicked will be there (Psalm 9:17a; I Corinthians 6:9,10; Revelation 21:8). All the moral, self-righteous people will be there (Matthew 7:21–23). All these will discover that hell is real, that it is not soul sleep, that death didn't end it all, that their punishment is everlasting, that there is no mercy there, that they are experiencing weeping and gnashing of teeth (Matthew 8:12), are crying for relief (Luke 16:24), are remembering the past (vs. 25), are looking across a great gulf (vs. 26), and are praying for lost loved ones back on earth. What a pity people have to go to hell before they become concerned for their lost loved ones on earth. It is too late then (vss. 27–31).

Some people are of the opinion that all the "hell" they will get is here on earth—that it is not a place. If there is a heaven—and there is, there has to be a hell because believer and unbeliever will not share both together. No evil will ever enter God's abode. If there is an *in*, there must be an *out*. If there is an *up*, there must be a *down*. Heaven is *up*, where Christ ascended. (Acts 1:11). Hell is from *beneath* (Isaiah 14:9a; Job 11:8).

We hear much today about "outer space," space ships going from to earth to the moon, Mars, Jupiter, etc. Very little is said about "inner space," which is below the earth's surface. An Associated Press writer, Lee Seigel, said that "in feeding data on earthquake shock waves into a computer produced what they call the most detailed "snapshots" yet of the earth's deep interior[61]

The earth's diameter is 8,000 miles. From its surface to the center it is 4,000 miles and is divided into four main parts.

1. The *Lithosphere* Zone, which is roughly 60 miles of soil, solid and fiery rock.
2. The *Mantle* Zone, which is about 940 miles of rock that flows under heated pressure, often producing earthquakes aud volcanic eruptions.
3. The *Intermediate* Zone, about 1,100 miles of iron content.
4. The *Centrosphere* Zone, the core of the earth, is about 4,000 miles thick, containing molten nickel and iron at 4,000 degrees Fahrenheit.

The Old Testament refers to sheol (hell) as the pit. The sons of Korah were swallowed up by an earthquake and went down into the *pit* (Numbers 16:33). The Psalmist refers to hell as *"the pit"* of destruction (55:23). We can glean from the fiery core of the earth and the earth swallowing the sons of Korah and their going down into the *pit*, that hell is located somewhere *in* the earth. Job, possibly the old-

The Principle of Judgment

est of all Bible books, contains at least forty up-to-date scientific facts, one of which agrees with the scientist's description of the inner earth. It relates to the earth as a place where the surface produces bread (food) and the under (inside) "is turned up as if it were fire" (25:8). This could also be interpreted that *deep down inside the earth there is eruption as by fire.* Job also makes it plain that those who have been ransomed do not go down into the *pit.* (33:24.27,28).

In a study of the awfulness of God's judgment for sinners who reject Christ as their Savior, the question is often asked, "How can a God of love send anyone to hell?" The answer is simple: "His love produced a love for their sin-sick soul by way of Christ's death at Calvary" to keep one from going there. If a person dies and goes to hell or the pit, they go because it is their choice, *their* unbelief in Christ.

The Bible makes it plain that God offers sinners an avenue of escape from a Christless eternity through His Son. The Holy Spirit engineers circumstances in such a way that the Gospel can be heard. Paul uses this argument in the First Chapter of Romans. He testifies that the Gospel of Christ is the power of God unto salvation to anyone who believes it. Belief implies repentance of sin and an acceptance of Christ by faith as their very own personal Savior (vss.16,17).

After Paul makes plain God's offer of the Gospel to all who will believe, he begins to paint a picture of their gross sins and points out that in their unbelief they will be without excuse when they face God in judgment (vss. 18–20). This is true of all sinners, whether the self-righteous (Matthew 7:21–23) or the out and out sinners as Paul describes in Romans. Some "change the glory of the incorruptible God into images of idols" (21–23). Unbelief says unto God, "Depart unto us for we do not desire the knowledge of God" (Job 21:14). Unbelief seeks to serve only self (vs. 24), and it exchanges the truth of God for a lie (vs. 25). Since God does not force anyone to believe and is not willing that any should perish, when they deliberately refuse truth, He gives them up. They turn to uncleanness, to affections under the possession of a reprobate mind and do and live what a depraved heart and mind desires. They know the judgment of God, knowing that such things are worthy of death, but have pleasure for a season in their sinful ways (vss. 24–32). The word *season* means *temporary* when compared to an eternity of reaping corruption.

We learn from Proverbs that when man refuses the Word of God as the Holy Spirit convicts of sin, God will laugh at their calamity when they set aside His counsel. God takes just so much from those who defy Him. When they do not fear the Lord, they shall eat of their own fruit which they sowed to the flesh, thus sealing their own doom. They will not be numbered among those who believe the Gospel and dwell in safety (1:23–33).

I'm sure you have heard it said that as long as there is life one can believe and be saved. The dying thief believed just before he died (Luke 23:23). I witnessed to a lady who was critically injured iii an automobile accident. She repeatedly refused to give her heart to the Lord. Seeing her lapse into a coma, she died before regaining consciousness. She had life in her body but in the coma it was impossible to believe.

It is possible for a sinner to have ample opportunity to believe and refuse one too many times. They can cross the "point of no return." Jesus brought out this truth. Because of the unbelief of the Pharisees, He said unto them, "I am from *above*, you are from *beneath*. I am from above and you are from this world. If you believe not that I am the Messiah, you shall die in your sins" (John 8:21–24). These unbelievers are given all opportunity to believe on Christ. What was the final outcome? Did they believe on Him while they had life or did they cross the point of ho return? Let's take a look at John 12:37–40. Jesus had performed many miracles before them to let them know He was the long anticipated Messiah. Yet they believed not on Him. They *could* have but refused over aud over the arm of the Lord which was outstretched to save them. By refusing Him over and over, not hearkening to His Word as we saw in Proverbs, they came to the point *where they could not believe*. Isaiah prophesied that there were those whose eyes would be blinded, that their hearts would not see and understand their need of Christ and be converted.

We ask the question again, "Does God send anyone to hell?" He loved every sinner so much that He spared not His own Son but delivered Him up for us all to give us freely salvation and all things (Romans 8:32). Just as Adam and Eve were given a choice to live or die spiritually, so God is not willing that any should perish. But if a sinner does die without Christ, "hell is God's one last act of love to people who will accept nothing else at His hand. God leaves one corner in the universe for which they can call their own, and in which they can continue to live for all eternity as though lie did not exist."[62]

2. The Judgment of Believers

Believers, like sinners, reap what they sow. If believers sow to the Spirit, benefits are reaped. If they sow to the flesh, judgment will follow. God will forgive when earnest repentance and confession is made, but consequences follow. David is an example of this with his affair with Bathsheba. He had an illicit affair with her and she became pregnant. To hide the affair that the baby was his, he got her husband drunk and then had him killed (II Samuel 11; Habakkuk 2:15). When Nathan, the prophet, gave a parable about a rich man who stole a lamb from a poor man, David's anger was kindled and said the rich man should restore the lamb "fourfold" and should die. Nathan told David "you are that man" (II Samuel 12:1–6). David confessed his sins to God and was forgiven. but the expression "fourfold" came back to haunt him because in judgment he lost four sons.

The most wise king Solomon obeyed the Lord in building the Temple but became most foolish when he worshiped idols with his idolatrous wives. When judgment befell him, the United Kingdom of Israel was divided into a Northern and Southern kingdom. Each was later defeated and people were taken into captivity (I Kings 11).

There was a Corinthian believer who was having an affair with either his mother or stepmother. The Church was to judge him to be delivered unto Satan for the destruction of his body that his soul would be saved in the day of the Lord Jesus (I Corinthians 5:1–5). This is a sin unto death (I John 5:16,17).

The Principle of Judgment

Unless the Lord's Supper (Communion) is observed obediently, there will be judgment. We are told prior to the partaking of the bread and the cup, we are to examine ourselves (I Corinthians 11:23–32). We must let the Holy Spirit search our hearts to reveal any unconfessed sin, even asking Him to reveal any secret faults or sin (Psalm 19:12). All should be forsaken and confessed, else those who cover their sins shall not prosper (Proverbs 28:13; I John 1:9). "If we judge ourselves we will not be judged but if we do not, God will judge us that we should not be condemned with the world (vss. 31,32). What, then, will our judgment be if we partake unworthily? Notice verses 28–30.

1. *Weakness*, due to lack of dedication. Hypocrisy begins to play a part and what spiritual strength we had in service is gone. We become something like the Corinthians—"babes in Christ" and not able to take a real stand for the Lord (I Corinthians 3:1,2). When Abraham gave Melchizedek tithes of all he possessed, Melehizedek gave him *bread* and unfermented *wine*, a symbol of Christ's broken body and the shedding of His blood (Genesis 14:18–20). I believe this is another time Abraham " saw Christ's day and rejoiced in it" (John 8:56). Could it be the reason so many believers are weak is because they do not tithe, yet partake of the Supper?

2. *Some form of sickness*. This can sideline an individual so that they are not playing an active role in serving the Lord. This is not to say that believers who are ill are being judged in partaking of the Supper unworthily, but it often happens to those who do not examine themselves worthily.

3. The last judgment mentioned is *"falling asleep"* or passing from this earthly scene. John tells us "there is a sin unto death" (I John 5:16,17). Here again this does not mean all who have become absent from the body and are present with the Lord failed the Communion test. But it is possible for those who constantly take it unworthily. We have already made note of the man who was judged with the destruction of his body that his spirit may be saved in the day of the Lord Jesus (I Corinthians 5:1–5).

The Apostle Paul was a spiritual giant. After being gloriously saved and making his first trip to Jerusalem. he was told to get out of this Jewish city. He was told to leave because the Jews would not hear him, saying, "Depart, for I will send you far from here unto the Gentiles." He was called the "Apostle to the uncircumcised or the Gentiles" (Acts 22:18–21; Romans 11:13).

Although he was used of God among the Gentiles, his heart was always heavy for his own kinsmen, the Jews. On one occasion he said "I could wish myself accursed [or separated] from Christ for my brethren, my kinsmen according to the flesh (Romans 9:3). He was as much as saying he would be willing to go to hell for the sake of the Jews to be saved. He knew that would be impossible, but he was expressing his love for his unsaved race. Never once did he make such a statement for those to whom he was called.

After his third missionary journey he was determined to go back to his favorite city, Jerusalem, the city from which he was to have removed himself. Accused of going into the Temple with a Gentile, he was all but torn limb from limb by despiteful Jews. Rescued by Roman soldiers, when it was discovered the Jews were plotting his life, he appealed to his Roman citizenship. This necessitated a trip to Rome to appear before Caesar. After a hectic voyage, he was in house arrest there for two years. I have often thought how much more Paul could have accomplished being free to go among the Gentiles as originally commanded by God. God always blesses his Word but sometimes must use judgment and withhold blessings if we are not completely in His will.

Believers must always remind themselves that God always welcomes his children when they humble themselves and repent of their sins. He will hear from heaven, forgive their sins and will cleanse them from all unrighteousness. The reason weakness, sickness and death befalls many is that they act like Cain. They are given opportunity to examine themselves and get right with God by doing the right thing but refuse to do it (Genesis 4:6,7).

3. The Judgment Seat of Christ

Jesus promised His followers He would come again and receive them unto Himself that where He is they would be also (John 14:2,3). Those who have died and will die before He returns are and will be absent from the body and present with Him (II Corinthians 5:8). When Jesus does return, "He will descend from heaven with a shout, with the voice of an archangel and with the trump of God. The dead in Christ will rise first, then we which are alive and remain shall be caught up together with them in the clouds to meet the Lord in the air and so shall we ever be with the Lord" (I Thessalonians 4:16,17). This is called the "Rapture of the Church." When this event takes place, "we must all appear before the Judgment Seat [Bema] of Christ. to receive what we deserve according to the deeds we have done while living on earth, whether good or bad[1]" (II Corinthians 5:10).

In our previous discussion we brought out that believers do sin. Even when confession is made and all is forgiven, consequences often linger as a result of judgment. The deeds we do that are good will be rewarded. Our bad deeds, because we did not confess them, will also be rewarded—not with gain but with loss. The believer does not work to be saved but he works because he is saved. He is to *work out* his salvation by obedience to God's Word (Philippians 2:12).

Having been saved to serve the Lord, we are held accountable for what we did and didn't do. having been raptured we are now facing Christ at his Judgment Seat (Bema). See First Corinthians 3:11–15. The foundation upon which we were to build or perform our deeds is Christ. All of our deeds will be tested by fire. If they were good and acceptable to the Lord, they will come forth as gold, silver and precious stones which cannot be damaged by fire. Such rewards are for—

- —Faithful service: Ruth 2:12.
- —Enduring persecution: Matthew 5:11,12.
- —Using our talents: Matthew 25:19–23.
- —Insignificant gifts: Mark 9:41.
- —Faithfulness—an incorruptible crown: I Corinthians 9:24,25.

The Principle of Judgment

—Bearing up under trials—a crown of life: James 1:12.
—Testifying, preaching the Word—a crown of glory: I Peter 5:1–4.
—Soul-winning—a crown of rejoicing: I Thessalonians 2:19,20.
—Loving Christ's appearing, looking for the Rapture—a crown of righteousness: II Timothy 4:8.

The result of good deeds passing the test of fiery judgment, the believer will hear his Savior say, "Well done good and faithful servant, enter into the joy of the Lord" (Matthew 25:21). Joy will also be manifested because of a "Book of Remembrance" God kept of those who feared Him. In addition to other rewards, *jewels* await the faithful saints (Malachi 3:16,17).

When the bad works or deeds are tested by fire at Christ's "Judgment Seat," the believer suffers loss. Everything, like wood, hay and stubble, is burned up with the individual receiving no rewards. However, the individual will be saved as one who escapes a fire. In heaven, yes, but nothing to show the Lord in appreciation for His salvation. What a tragedy to be in heaven with Christ empty-handed but at least "saved by grace!"

4. The Great White Throne Judgment

This is God's final judgment and it is for all the unsaved of all ages, beginning, no doubt, with Cain. Revelation 20:11–15 gives us the picture of this judgment. God, having kept records of all humans, opens His record books, one of which is called the "Book of Life" which records the names of the redeemed of all ages. No believer will stand before God at this judgment. No believer will have his name erased. Notice that the record for Christians is singular—book. This, no doubt, is because few there be who were on the straight and narrow way.

Because many are on the broad road leading to destruction, their record is such that books, plural, had to be used. This is God's final judgment for all the "great and small" dead sinners from the beginning of time. The sea, hell and the grave give up the dead and all are now resurrected—resurrected to judgment or condemnation (John 5:29). Each will be judged by his or her own works or actions (Matthew 16:27), their words (Matthew 12:37), and their thoughts or secrets (Romans 2:16; Luke 8:17). Each will be compared and judged by God's righteousness and holy standard, and each will be found wanting because they sinned and came short of God's glory (Romans 3:23). Those whose name are not found in the "Book of Life" will be cast into the "lake of fire," along with Satan.

A New Heaven and A New Earth

At the close of the "Great White Throne Judgment," God will have wiped away all sin from the earth and ushered in a new Heaven and a new earth wherein dwells righteousness (Revelation 21:1–4; II Peter 3:13). The last two chapters of Revelation (21,22), give us a description of this new home for the children of God for all ages.

SUMMARY

We have considered four judgments of God in this Chapter. The first referred to Christ rejecters who have died or will die in their sin and go to hell. The second has to do with believers reaping what they sowed or are sowing—not only good seeds but bad, sinful ones. The third deals with the Judgment Seat of Christ, believers before Christ receiving rewards for good works and suffering loss for bad ones. The fourth, the Great White Throne, for all the unsaved of all ages standing before God with the "gleaming brightness of His glory and infinite holiness showing up every sin in their lives, where they cannot hide a thing.[63] Their sin had been hidden all these years but now they are revealed at last. Sin cannot be hidden (Job 34:22).

The late Dr. Harry Rimmer, a noted scholar and Bible teacher gave us a beautiful picture of that wonderful place called heaven where all the redeemed of all ages will spend eternity with their Heavenly Father and their wonderful Savior, Jesus Christ.

Heaven, I'm Going There

"I'm interested in that Land because I have a clear title to a bit of property there. I did not buy it. It was given to me 'without money and without price.' But the Donor purchased it for me at a tremendous price, a tremendous sacrifice. I am riot holding it for speculation since the title is non-transferable. It is not a vacant lot. "Ever since I was saved, I have been sending up material out of which the Master Architect and Builder of our vast universe has been building a home for me, a home that will never be remodeled nor repaired because it will suit me perfectly, and will never, never grow old. Termites can never undermine its foundation, for it rests upon the 'Rock of Ages.' A fire cannot destroy it. Floods cannot wash it away. Earthquakes cannot crush it nor can tornados blow it away. No locks nor bolts will ever be placed on its doors for no vicious person can ever enter that Land where my dwelling stands—now nearer completion than when I first believed. When I go to meet my Savior—absent from the body to be present with the Lord, it will be ready for me to enter and abide in peace eternally, without any fear of ever being evicted!

"There is a valley of deep shadows between the place where I now live and the place to which I shall journey—maybe sooner than I think . I cannot reach my home in that City of God without passing through this dark valley of shadows (unless I am raptured first); but I am not afraid, because the best Friend I ever had went through this same valley long, long ago, alone, and drove away all its gloom. He has stuck with me through thick and thin since we first became acquainted, and I have his promise in printed form that He will never leave me nor forsake me, that He will be with me always, never to be left alone! He will be with me as I walk through the valley of the shadow of death, and I shall not lose my way because He is with me.

"I have no assurance I will be here another day—that I will hear another sermon on 'heaven.' My ticket to heaven has no date marked for this journey, no return coupon, and no permit for any baggage. Yes, I am ready to die. And I shall look forward to meeting all my loved ones in Christ over there some day. Best of all is seeing My Savior and becoming as He is.

"For those of you who might not be saved and are not prepared to die and meet the Lord, please talk to my pastor after my funeral, and find out how, through the Lord Jesus Christ, you can meet me over there in heaven."

Sometime ago I ran across a heart-warming devotional written in 1849 by a Rev. James Smith of London. I can't think of no better thought to close this chapter than its message—We Shall See him as He Is (I John 3:2).

We never saw the "Man of Sorrows" in his humiliation, but we shall see him in his glorified state. He will soon revisit our heavens . Then we shall be caught up in the clouds and see Him. As we gaze upon Him we shall be made like him. Every spot or trace of imperfection in us will be forever done away as this corruptible is changed to incorruption. When we see Him our love will be made perfect, our admiration abiding and our joy complete. We shall be with Him sharing His joys, gracing his triumphs, and inheriting His fulness. We shall never lose sight of Him for He will dwell with us and we shall always be delighted with his love. Now we see him by faith, aud whom having not seen we love. how truly sweet aud precious this is. We may often mourn at a distance for him and long and cry, "0 to see his face!" Yes, now we are the children of God and it does not yet appear what we shall be, but we do know that when He will appear, we shall be just Him! All sighing, crying, tears aud desiring has ended, and all will be satisfaction, joy and peace.

A Prayer Thought

Dear Lord, with the blessed hope of Christ's returning for his saints on the Horizon, may I be doing what I should be doing, going where I should be going, thinking and saying what I should be saying either when I fall asleep in Him or if I am alive when He comes in the clouds to take me to be with himself. In Your name I pray. Amen.

(II Timothy 4:8; Revelation 22:20)

ENDNOTES

1. Bob Boyd, *Clip 'n Save*, Martin Printers, Lancaster, PA, 1963 (pg. 5)
2. F. B. Meyer, *Clip 'n Save*, (pg. 11)
3. Robert T. Boyd, *Born to Die*, World Bible Publishers, Iowa City, IA, 1997, (pg. 22)
4. *Clip 'n Save*, (pg. 24)
5. Robert T. Boyd, *World's Bible Handbook*, World Pub., 1991 (pg. 29).
6. Ibid., (pg. 29)
7. E. H. Bancroft, *Elemental Theology*, Conservative Book and Bible Pub., Binghamton, NY, (pg. 33)
8. Evangelist Robertson, *The Evangelist*, Chattanooga, TN (pg. 34)
9. Adam Clarke, *Clarke's Commentary, Vol V*, Abingron-Cokesbury Press, Nashville, TN (pg. 37)
10. John MacArthur, *The MacArthur Study Bible*, Word Bibles, Nashville, TN (pg. 39)
11. *World's Bible Handbook*, (pg. 39)
12. Ibid., (pg. 42)
13, 14. Ibid., (pg. 42)
15. Ibid., (pg. 49)
16. Rev. Ravenhill (pg. 51)
17. *Clip 'n Save* (pg. 55)
18, 19. World's Bible Handbook (pgs. 56, 57)
20. Ibid., (pg. 57)
21. E. M. Bounds, *Power Through Prayer*, Marshall Bros., London (pg. 58)
22. *World's Bible Handbook* (pg. 59)
23. Frances L. Boyd, *Language of Prayer*, (pg. 60)
24. Keith L. Brooks, *Prayer Points* (pg. 61)
25. Harry Rimmer, *The Golden Text for Today*, Van Kampen Press, Wheaton, IL, 1951 (pg. 65)
26. *World's Bible Handbook* (pg. 67)
27. Ibid. (pg. 68)
28. Ibid. (pg. 68)
29, 30. Ibid. (pgs. 72, 73)
31. Adam Clarke, *Vol. V* (pg. 81)

32. Ibid. (pg. 81)
33. Lois Kendall Blanchard (pg. 83)
34. Adam Clarke *Vol. V* (pg. 87)
35. *World's Bible Handbook* (pg. 88)
36. Ibid. (pg. 89)
37. Ibid. (pg. 91)
38. Ibid. (pg. 92)
39. Adam Clarke, *Vol. V* (pg. 94)
40. *World's Bible Handbook* (pg. 96)
41. Ibid. (pg. 97)
42. Bob Boyd, *Now Hear This*, Martin Printers (pg. 98)
43. C. H. Towne, *Clip 'n Save* (pg. 102)
44. Herbert W. Yovey, *A Passion for Souls*, Al Smith Pub., Greenville, SC, 1914, (pg. 107).
45. *Clip 'n Save* (pg. 110)
46. Ibid. (pg. 112)
47. Rev. James Smith, *Daily Bible Readings*, American Baptist Pub., Philadelphia, PA, 1849 (pg. 113)
48. Jews for Jesus, *Thanksgiving Letter*, Nov. 1998, San Francisco, CA (pg. 117).
49. *Clip 'n Save* (pg. 117)
50. Dr. Herbert Arnold, *Denbigh (VA) Baptist Dispatch*, Nov. 1998 (pg. 118)
51. Jews for Jesus (pg. 121)
52. *Clip 'n Save* (pg. 122)
53. Ibid. (pg. 123)
54. Isaac Watts, *When I Survey the Wondrous Cross*, (pg. 124)
55. Clarke, Adam, *Vol.VI* (pg. 127)
56. Telford, Dr. Andrew, *Ephesians*, 1982 (pg. 130)
57. Beachy, Dwight, *My Father's House, a House of Prayer*, Christian Light Publications, Harrisonburg, VA (pg. 131)
58. World's Bible Handbook (pg. 132)
59. Stanley, Dr. Charles, *Lessons from Life of David*, In Touch, Atlanta, GA, July, 1999 (pg. 132)
60. *Clip 'n Save*, (pg. 135)
61. Seigel, Lee, *Associated Daily Press*, NY, May 4, 1984 (pg. 136)
62. *Clip 'n Save*, (pg. 138)
63. Turner, Pastor Marvin, *Book of Revelation* (pg. 142).

BIBLIOGRAPHY

American Standard (New) Bible, Thomas Nelson Pub., Nashville, TN, 1985
Amplified Bible, The, Zondervan Pub. [louse, Grand Rapids, MI, 1965
Bancroft, E. H., Elemental Theology, Bible Pub., Co., Binghamton, NY 1932
Bounds, E. M., Power Through Prayer, Marshall Bros., Ltd., London
Boyd, Robert T., World's Bible Handbook, World Bible Pub., Iowa Falls, Iowa, 1991
   Ibid. The Apostle Paul, World Bible Pub., 1995
   Ibid. Born to Die, Understanding Christ's Life, World, 1997
   Ibid. Boyd's Handbook of Practical Apologetics, Kregel Publications, Grand Rapids, MI 1997
Boyd, Bob, Clip 'n Save, Drake Printing Co., Johnson City, NY, 1961
   Ibid. Now Hear This, Martin Printing Co., Lancaster, PA, 1967
   Ibid. Good Morning Lord, Martin, 1965
Chambers, Oswald, My Utmost for His Highest, Dodd, Mead & Co., NY 1935
Clarke's, Adam, Commentary, Vol V, Abingdon-Cokesbury Press, Nashville, TN
Douglas, J. S, Tenney, Merrill, The New International Dictionary of the Bible, Zondervan, 1987
Estep, Howard, The Seed of Abraham, World Prophetic Ministry, Colton, Ca, 1979
Foreman, Kenneth, Jr., Hunter, Archiball M. , Love, Julian Price,
The Layman's Bible Commentary, John Knox Press, Richmond, VA, 1959
Knox, Msgr. Ronald, Translation of Latin Vulgate Bible into Modern English, Sheed & Ward, NY, 1950
MacArthur, John, MacArthur Study Bible, Word Bible, Nashville, TN, 1997
Marshall, Cathrine, The Prayers of Peter Marshall, McGraw-Hill Book Co., Inc., NY 1949
New International Holy Bible (NIV), Zondervan, 1978
Richards, Lawrence O., Expository Dictionary of Bible Words, Zondervan, 1988
Rimmer, Harry, The Purposes of Calvary, Wm. B. Eerdmans, Grand Rapids, MI, 1939
   Ibid. The Magnificence of Jesus, Zondervan, 1943
   Ibid. The Golden Text for Today, Van Kampen Press, Wheaton, IL, 1950
Ryrie, Charles C., The Ryrie Study Bible, Moody Press, Chicago, IL, 1976
Scofield Reference Bible (New), Oxford Press, NY, 1967

Smith, Rev. James, Daily Bible Readings, American Baptist Pub. Society, Philadelphia, 1849
Strauss, Lehman, Sense and Nonsense of Prayer, Moody Press, 1974
Telford, Andrew, Studies in Ephesians, 1982
Turner, Marvin V., The Book of Revelation, 1960
Vines Expanded Expository Dictionary of New Testament Words, Bethany House Pub., Minneapolis, MN, 1984
Water, Mark, Knowing God's Will, Hendrickson Pub., Peabody, MA, 1998
Weirsbe, Warren W., Be Free (Galatians), Victory Books. Wheaton, IL, 1979
Wilson's Old Testament Studies, MacDonald Pub., McLean, VA
Wuest, Kenneth S., Expanded Translation of the Greek New Testament, Wm. B. Eerdmans, 1958